WAR IN EUROPE

"One day President Roosevelt told me that he was asking publicly for suggestions about what the war should be called. I said at once, 'the unnecessary war.' There never was a war more easy to stop than that which had just wrecked what was left of the world from the previous struggle... The human tragedy reaches its climax in the fact that after all the exertion and sacrifices of hundreds of millions of people and the victors of the Righteous Cause, we still have not found Peace or Security, and that we lie in the grip of even worse perils than those we have surmounted."

—Winston Churchill
The Gathering Storm

WAR IN EUROPE

SIDNEY C. MOODY JR.
and The Associated Press

★
PRESIDIO

Copyright © 1993 The Associated Press
Published by Presidio Press
505 B San Marin Dr., Suite 300
Novato, CA 94945-1340

Editor: Norm Goldstein
Photo Researcher: Kieran Eustace
News Library Researcher: Arnold Wilkinson

Designed by: Combined Books, 151 E. 10th Ave., Conshohocken, PA 19428

Library of Congress Cataloging-in-Publication Data
Moody, Sidney C.
    War in Europe / Sidney C. Moody Jr., The Associated Press.
        p.   cm.
    Includes bibliographical references.
    ISBN 0-89141-494-0
    1. World War, 1939-1945 — Campaigns — Europe. 2. World War, 1939-1945 — Campaigns—Europe—Pictorial works. I. Associated Press. II. Title.
D756.M585   1993
940.54'21—dc20   93-23095
                                                                    CIP
Printed in the United States of America.

Illustration for Half-Title: *While Paris gendarmes looked on, German troops marched in triumph down the Champs Elysees.*

Illustration for Title Page: *After the Jews revolted against their Nazi oppressors, all that remained of the Warsaw ghetto was a ruined Catholic church, part of the ghetto wall and the ghosts of almost 500,000 murdered Jews.*

Illustration, this page: *Door by door American paratroopers hunted out Germans in the remains of St. Mere Eglise in Normandy.*

Contents

Above: *A master of spectacle, Hitler mesmerized the German people with mass rallies such as this in Berlin in 1934 at Tempelhof airdrome with 2 million followers.*

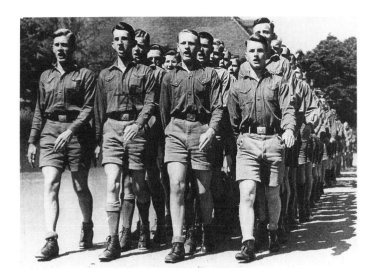

1

Versailles

It is May 1940, in France, near Raucourt four miles south of Sedan. A company commander of Germany's 10th Panzer Division muses during a lull to his tankmates.

His grandfather had been killed at Sedan during the Franco-Prussian War in 1871. His father had been killed near there in World War I. "If I die, this is the end of a military clan." A French shell explodes near his head. The prophesy is fulfilled.

Facing Page: *The two-way railroad car. Marshal Ferdinand Foch, fourth from left with briefcase, leaves car in Compiegne after Germany's World War I surrender. Twenty-two years later Hitler dictated terms to the fallen French in the same car.*

Above: *While the rest of the world wrestled with economic collapse, the Hitler Youth mobilized as soldiers of tomorrow.*

Thus, World War II.

Winston Churchill called it "the unnecessary war." Yes.

* * * *

It is no bookkeeping convenience that the world wars of the 20th century, like Super Bowls, bear sequential Roman numerals. It is literal and symbolic fact that blood spilled at Verdun in 1917 could have sired blood spilled in Normandy in 1944. I germinated II through the fatal seed of the Treaty of Versailles which did — but did not — end the first world war.

The treaty changed the balance and the map of Europe. In 1917 czarist Russia, bled white by battle, became a train wreck from which emerged the Soviet Union. The shadow of communism was far more threatening than the Russian bear had ever been.

The Austro-Hungarian Empire dissolved from senescence and a nationalism championed by Presi-

dent Woodrow Wilson of the United States. The various Versailles treaties gave birth to new states — Yugoslavia, Hungary, Czechoslovakia — and an independent Poland. They were to become pawns in a scramble for security among the Powers. Or revenge.

Revenge because the triumphant winners, Britain and France, attached the whole blame for the cataclysm on Germany. East Prussia was cut off from the Fatherland to give Poland a corridor to the Baltic Sea at Danzig. Germany was stripped of its overseas colonies. And the victors levied crushing reparations on their beaten foe. Blunders, miscalculation, national egotism and naivete had marked Europe's descent into World War I. The blame could have been shared all around, but Versailles did not do so. To Germany the treaty was a Diktat, an unjust

Left: *An elderly Berlin Jew tries to reason before the killing made words pointless.*

Below: *As early as 1935 the Nazis put on a display of armored warfare at a party rally in Nuremberg. Tank cannons contravened terms of the Treaty of Versailles that ended World War I.*

arm-twisting that became a focal point for nationalist emotions. Lloyd George, Britain's doughty wartime prime minister whose hands were not all that clean, nonetheless guessed the future and lived long enough to see it:

"...If (Germany) feels she has been unjustly treated in the peace of 1919, she will find means of extracting retribution from her conquerors."

At first this seemed unlikely. Postwar Germany became a bloody battleground between private armies of communists and the right-wing Freikorps. Out of it emerged the Weimar Republic. This had all the best intentions in the world but few of the leaders and experience to make them work. Furthermore, it was ever tainted by the stain of its Versailles parentage. Right off it was beset by an inflationary collapse of the economy overburdened by reparations.

By 1923, one egg in Germany cost 30 million marks. The government printed all but worthless 20 billion mark notes. A worker took a trolley to a bank to deposit his paycheck to find it had devalued by three-quarters by the time he arrived at the cashier's window. A housewife went shopping with a basketful of money. Thieves accosted her, threw the money in the gutter and took the basket.

Versailles limited the German army to 100,000

In 1933, Hitler, a decorated corporal in World War I, succeeded Paul von Hindenberg, military commander in that war, as Chancellor of Germany.

men. It forbade Germany making any tracked vehicles. It could make armored cars with turrets, but they could not contain guns. But the year after the Allied Control Commission left Germany in 1927, Krupp began making tanks. The parts were clandestinely shipped to Russia where German soldiers trained with them. German pilots were also flying there. Crash victims were sent home in crates marked as "spare parts." Glider clubs sprang up where young Germans learned to fly under the guise of sport. Lufthansa, the new national airline, trained other pilots who flew transports easily converted to bombers.

The director of this secret rearmament was Col. General Hans von Seeckt, who handpicked recruits to his small army to train as a cadre of officers and noncoms. Von Seeckt was a close reader of the English military analyst and visionary B.H. Liddell Hart who saw in the primitive World War I tank the coming breakthrough weapon. As the tank would outpace the foot soldier so the dive bomber would supplant artillery. It could strike from a distance by surprise without announcing its presence with a

W.C.

In 1929, a disgruntled SS trooper planted a bomb and himself under a podium where Hitler was to speak. Leaving to relieve himself, the soldier was inadvertently locked in the men's water closet. It was the first of many of Hitler's miraculous escapes from assassination.

Right: *Hitler's Brown Shirts heil their Fuhrer after he took office as Chancellor in 1933. They would soon feel his wrath.*

Under red, white and black swastika flags —the "crooked cross"—young Germans learned the heady mythology of Aryan supremacy.

barrage. The Germans would call their new strategy "blitzkrieg" — lightning war.

There was another hidden alliance between two intrinsic enemies. In the 1920s, Germany and Russia ran a joint factory at Bersol outside Moscow. It made poison gas.

The disorder within Germany was echoed beyond its borders. The French, population 39 million, could no longer embrace a politically unpalatable communist Russia to encircle Germany, population 59 million. Haunted by memories of the slaughter of Verdun — as was Britain by the Somme where 60,000 of its finest youth were shot down in a day — France sought alliances among the new nations of central Europe in a patchwork of treaties and negotiations.

Into this discord — a nervous France, an unknown communist colossus, a new Europe groping its way and a vengeful but weak Germany — slid an obscure Austrian who would determine as per-

haps no other a century of isms. Churchill was to call him a "guttersnipe." Adolf Hitler had, in fact, once been just that.

In 1939, Erich Kordt of the German Foreign Office was to say: "Only a single man wanted war." It is sustainable to say that a single man got his will and his wish. But it was in the context of the ruin of World War I. Cause and effect.

Hitler was born April 20, 1889, in Branau, Austria. His father, Alois Shicklgruber, was illegitimate and took the name Hitler, a variant on the surname of his stepfather. A teacher remembered young Adolf as "willful, arrogant, irascible...lazy...demanded of his fellow pupils unqualified subservience." His half-brother Alois Jr. said: "If he didn't get his way, he got very angry."

As a youth he migrated to Vienna where he thought he had more talent as an artist-architect than did the academies that turned him down. He lived near the lower depths, even begging at one

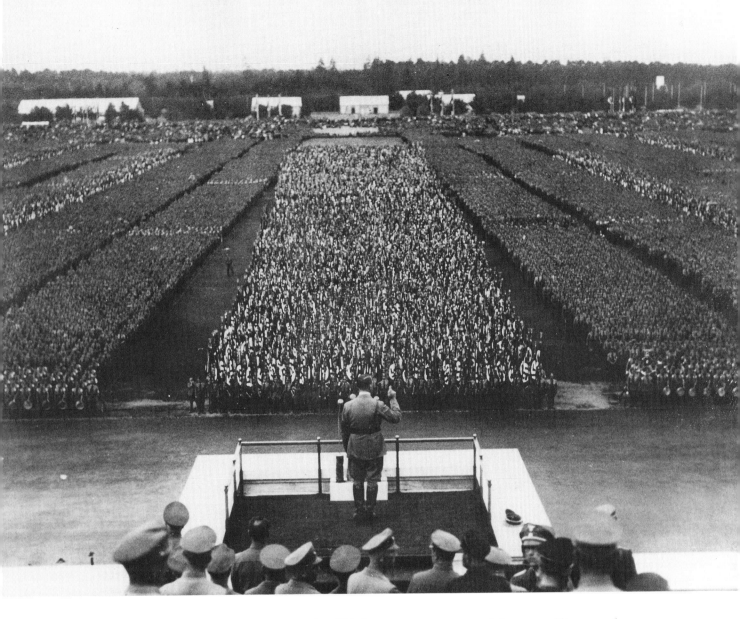

To the strains of heroic Wagnerian music, Hitler stage-managed huge rallies such as this in 1935 at Nuremberg, haranguing Germans to avenge the defeat of World War I.

point, and roomed in cheap hostels where he painted, talked politics and was rather liked by his fellow boarders. He moved to Munich, ducked the military draft but signed up when the war began in 1914. He was a brave and decorated runner for his regiment, was wounded in the thigh and gassed and never went beyond corporal, both by choice and "lack of leadership," said his superiors.

He returned to Munich after the war and worked for the military, infiltrating tiny splinter parties that foamed up and went flat by the dozens in the beer halls of a politically unstable city. In 1921, at his own insistence, he became head of such a group that met at the Burgerbraukeller: the Nationalist Socialist German Workers Party, Nazi for short. The party flaunted a black, red and white flag, designed by a member dentist, centered by a swastika, an ancient emblem of the Teutonic Knights and an older Sanskrit symbol meaning "all is all."

A High Heil

Berlin hosted the 1936 Olympics where many U.S. athletes including Harvard oarsman Bill Haskins refused to shake the Fuhrer's hand. Hitler did congratulate German Hans Wolke for winning the shotput. The International Olympic Committee ruled he would have to congratulate all winners or none. Hitler chose none. But Jesse Owens said Hitler did wave after the black American sprinter won four gold medals.

Hitler discovered a genius for oratory, drawing adherents with impassioned attacks on Jews and Communists for the "stab in the back" rioting back home that he charged, as did many others, led to the army's defeat in 1918. He had found a scapegoat for Germany's troubles and an audience willing to listen.

On November 7, 1923, Hitler, dressed in a cutaway like a bridegroom, sipped a beer (1 billion marks a glass) with Ernst Hanfstaengl, a Harvard graduate and descendant of two American Civil War generals. Then he climbed a table in the Burgerbraukeller, fired two shots into the ceiling for attention, and led his private army, the SA or Brown Shirts, on city hall to take over the government. Eighteen Nazis and three policemen were killed in the ensuing riot. Hitler fled to the Hanfstaengl's villa where he was arrested after Frau Hanfstaengl took away his pistol for fear he would kill himself.

Taken to prison where he was treated like a privileged guest, Hitler began writing his testament, "Mein Kampf" (My Struggle). It rambles but leaves no doubt as to the author's intentions: "...(my aim) is to secure for the German people the land and soil to which they are entitled on this earth...(We) turn our gaze towards the east (where Russia has fallen) under the yoke of the Jew..." "...There is no such thing as coming to an understanding with the Jews. I must be hard and fast. 'Either-or.'"

His guards were converted by this new Messiah and let him keep his light on until midnight, writing. In time the magnetism of his message and the brute

At monster rallies and parades, young soldiers of the new German army came, saw— and believed.

force of his SA made Hitler the dominant power in Germany. He became Chancellor January 30, 1933, four weeks before Franklin D. Roosevelt became President of the United States. As Hitler took office a Jewish lad named Leslie Frankel was skating near Worms. "Even as kids of 10, we shook."

Fate played into Hitler's hands almost at once. On February 27, 1933, Germany's parliament, the Reichstag, burned down. The Nazis blamed the communists. Hitler dismissed all Jews from the civil service. March 9 a "concentration camp" was opened at Dachau. Nine days later a Jew, Siegbert Kindermann, was beaten to death by storm troopers. His body, a swastika carved in its chest, was discarded out a window. Next month four Jews were shot at the camp without warning. By 1935, 75,000 of Germany's half-million Jews had emigrated. In September 1935 the Nuremberg Laws deprived Jews of German citizenship. But borrowing from Friedrich Nietzsche and his philosophy of the superman, Hitler played Pied Piper to his self-styled pure-blood Aryan people with Wagnerian spectacles, youth camps and mesmerizing speeches of conquest for Lebensraum — living space — from inferior peoples.

Nietzsche himself had written: "Intoxication means more to the Germans than nourishment ... A popular leader must hold up before them the prospect of conquest and splendor, then he will be believed." Germans believed.

They believed when Hitler's field-gray troops marched into Austria unopposed March 12, 1938.

"Winter Exercise" 1936

Hitler picked a Saturday, March 7, 1936, to occupy the Rhineland, the area between the French border and the Rhine demilitarized by Versailles. The British government would be weekending. King Edward VIII had just assumed the British throne. He had talked privately of accord with Germany. The League of Nations had vacillated about Italy's conquest of Ethiopia. Anthony Eden was to write in his memoirs: "Not one man in a thousand in Britain was prepared to oppose occupation." France was the worry.

Hitler sent three battalions across the Rhine in Operation Winter Exercise with orders to withdraw immediately if France reacted with force. It did not. In two days, 25,000 German soldiers stood on the forbidden ground. "It was the most nerve-racking night of my life," Hitler admitted. Lord Lothian said in Britain after the weekend: "The Germans, after all, are only going into their own back garden."

Hitler went to his boyhood home of Linz to declare the "reunification of the Germanic peoples (Anschluss)." France and Britain protested. But that is all they did. Five hundred Austrian Jews committed suicide.

2

"GREEN"

1938

Versailles had left Czechoslovakia poised like a geographical knife into the eastern innards of Germany. Anschluss, with the addition of Austria to the Third Reich, made the penetration even deeper. To the west, in France, was a wall. It was the

Above: *British Prime Minister Neville Chamberlain, left, thought he won "peace for our time" from Hitler at Munich. "The government had to choose between shame and war, "scoffed Winston Churchill. "They chose shame and will get war."*

Left: Hitler outlines his demands for lebensraum—living space—in Eastern Europe in an address to the Reichstag in 1938. No. 2 Nazi, Hermann Goering, behind the Fuhrer, then threatened use of his Luftwaffe planes to defend "rights" of German minorities.

Maginot Line, in-depth fortifications stretching from Switzerland to Luxembourg. Like many walls, it shut out reality and afforded false security.

France began building it in 1930. Aptly, it was named for a World War I war minister, Andre Maginot. Aptly, for it represented an all-too-recurring military mindset: to fight the next war in terms of the last. Verdun, where 700,000 soldiers had fallen to little avail and where the land was still unnaturally upheaved and pitted, was branded on the French psyche to the point of being a state of mind. Never again.

The Maginot Line would be a prefabricated assurance that Verdun would not recur. It was preceded by barbed wire and tank traps, then casements reinforced by 10 feet of concrete, then, every three or five miles, forts. The forts could hold up to 12,000 men each. They had subterranean gyms and barracks and hospitals and cinemas and generators and air conditioning and food and ammunition for three months. It was hideously expensive, one reason why it was not continued along the French-Belgian border to the English Channel. Another reason was that the extension would disrupt large industrial centers in its path. And it would make Belgium, where Germany's Schlieffen Plan had first struck in World War I, feel abandoned. A nicety considering that Belgium's King Leopold III had declared his country's neutrality in 1935. Maginot was an imposing defense, and Germany had no equivalent. But, unfortunately, it could not move.

In France's footsteps, Czechoslovakia had also built extensive fortifications along its German border, backed up by a considerable arms industry. Again unfortunately, the militarized zones of the new nation were also home to 3.5 million ethnic Germans, the Sudetens. Having bluffed twice in the Rhineland and Austria, Hitler upped the ante by demanding the "rights" of the Sudeten Germans be protected.

Hermann Goering, head of the Luftwaffe, Hitler's air force, a World War I ace and corpulent sybarite of Nazidom, blustered: "The Czechs are (a) ... vile race of dwarfs ... and behind them ... there can be seen the everlasting face of the Jewish fiend." Hitler backed up the rhetoric by putting 500,000 men under Fritz Todt to work building the Siegfried Line opposite the Maginot. Gen. Ludwig Beck, chief of staff of the OKW, the German high command, protested that war would be a "catastrophe." Hitler replied that "every generation must experience war once." Beck, who reasoned once had been enough, quit and became head of a generals' conspiracy against Hitler. Undeterred, Hitler ordered Plan Green, the invasion of the Sudetenland, be ready for October 1, 1938. Europe panicked.

Another politician summed up Britain's Prime Minister Neville Chamberlain as "a good town clerk in Birmingham in a lean year." Nevertheless, he flew (his first long flight) to the Berghof, Hitler's alpine Bavarian retreat, to try and reason together. While an ominous storm rattled the picture windows, Hitler ranted: "I shall settle the question one way or another!" Chamberlain proposed self-determination for the Sudetens. Hitler seemed amenable and the Prime Minister flew home to consult his allies. He felt sure, he wrote his sister, that Hitler could be trusted "when he has given his word."

When the Englishman returned in a few days to

Neville Chamberlain yielded Czechoslovakia to Hitler at Munich in 1938 without even asking the Czechs to the conference.

Bad Godesberg on the Rhine to tell Hitler of the Allies' acceptance, Hitler stunned him: "I am exceedingly sorry, but that (self-determination) is no longer any use." Chamberlain flew home in a tizzy. Germany was mobilizing, France partially so. Britain didn't have much to mobilize besides the fleet. The Allies might have better realized what sort of game they were playing had they stood with Hitler at his Chancellery window in Berlin as he dourly contemplated a downcast crowd watch a division marching through the city to the front. "I can't wage war with this nation (Germany) yet," he said.

Right: Nazi legions display their banners of terror.

In revenge for the murder of a German diplomat in Paris, German authorities unleashed Kristallnacht November 9-10, 1938. Some 267 synagogues were plundered and 815 shops wrecked in an orgy of blood and broken glass.

"KRISTALLNACHT"

1938

On November 6, 1938, one Hirschel Grynszpan, angered that his Jewish father had been whipped and deported from Germany, walked into the German embassy in Paris and shot and killed the first diplomat he found. A knowing Hitler looked the other way three nights later when underlings ordered security police to retaliate. Some 200 synagogues and 800 Jewish-owned shops were burned, 91 Jews killed and 20,000 "disappeared." Jews were fined 1 billion marks, and Jewish children barred from schools. An English reporter watched what came to be called "Crystal Night" because of all the broken glass. Asked what he was doing, he replied:

"Observing German culture."

Across the Channel, Chamberlain confessed: "I'm wobbling all over the place." At the last minute, Benito Mussolini, Germany's comic opera Axis partner in Italy, arranged a meeting in Munich. Invited were the two dictators, Chamberlain and Prime Minister Edouard Daladier of France. Jan Masaryk, Czech ambassador in London, asked if his country would be represented. No.

On September 29, the Allies agreed to turn over Sudetenland to Germany. An elated Chamberlain, thinking he had brought "peace for our time," returned to London to break the good news to Parliament. (He forgot his famous umbrella back at Munich.) In the galleries of the House of Commons, Queen Mary burst into tears of relief. Former Prime Minister Stanley Baldwin thumped his cane and the Archbishop of Canterbury pounded the railing in approval. Churchill, long consigned to the back of the bus of British politics, stalked out with scathing prescience: "The government had to choose between shame and war. They chose shame, and will get war."

In Paris, Cardinal Verdier refused to ring the bells of Notre Dame cathedral in celebration. They would remain silent in mourning, he said.

"We got everything we wanted just like that," chortled Goering with a snap of his fingers.

It was foregone the following March when Germany marched again, taking over Moravia and Bohemia in Czechoslovakia as "protectorates," leaving Slovakia "independent." Russia proposed a six-power conference to stop Hitler. Chamberlain said it would be "premature."

Hitler threw in another chip, this time Poland, its "oppressed" German minorities and particularly the Versailles-created Danzig corridor that isolated East Prussia. But it was not all bombast. Germany had long had mail planes, even back in the disarmed days, that were swifter than the fastest French fighters. Now he had the Junkers-87 "Stuka," a dive bomber equipped with a terrifying siren, "The Trumpet of Jericho," which shrieked as the plane plummeted on its target. But fatal indications of hubris had crept in. In a blitzkrieg lasting a few weeks, there would be no need for heavy bombers. So Hitler ordered none. Nor did he see any need to increase the short range of his otherwise very adequate Messerschmitt-109 fighters. This would cost him.

He made another miscalculation if bluff were his game. After the occupation of Czechoslovakia, Chamberlain began to draw a line. Hitler believed: "The British will leave the Poles in the lurch as they did the Czechs." But Chamberlain and Daladier pledged Warsaw "full support" if its independence were threatened. Appeasement, too late, was over. As a counterplot, Hitler pondered an unthinkable partnership with the high priest of communism, Josef Stalin. The players, with the notable exception of the United States, were assembling.

"AMOS & ANDY"

1930s

Regular as clockwork, once a week in the '30s in America, phone calls abruptly plummeted by 50 percent. Thirty million Americans were tuning into "Amos & Andy" on the parlor radio.

Maybe it was a Philco or a Stromberg-Carlson, mysterious things with tubes that glowed orange inside elaborately machined wooden cases with fluted legs and fancy columns and arches just like the church down the street. The analogy fits. The radio had become the family icon. Its role in drawing the United States into Europe's affairs was subtle — not as powerful as television and Vietnam — but it should not be underestimated.

Above: *Gen. George C. Marshall was called "the architect of victory." He was.*

Left: His gamble at Munich won, Hitler tours the newly-occupied Sudeten region of dismembered Czechoslovakia.

Ladies' afternoon bridge clubs dropped their cards and leaned forward to hear through the static Edward VIII abdicate his throne in 1936 "for the woman I love." Correspondents, live, told of Mussolini's invasion of Ethiopia in 1935, of the Spanish Civil War in 1936. Americans snuggled aloofly between their comforting oceans, but they couldn't shut out the airwaves. You could hear, also live, Adolf Hitler ranting and there was William L. Shirer to tell you what he was saying if you didn't understand German.

The power of radio was unintentionally demonstrated by Orson Welles' "War of the Worlds" broadcast, a caper meant to brighten up Halloween 1938. New Jersey, where Welles' "Martians" landed for reasons best known to themselves, went berserk.

Radio's impact was hardly less several years later when you could hear in your living room the ack-ack and exploding bombs of the London blitz and Edward R. Murrow intoning, "This [pause] is London." Americans were becoming ear-witnesses to the world.

Not that they didn't have problems enough at home. Millions were still out of work in an endless Depression and the High Plains blew away in the Dust Bowl winds and John Steinbeck told all about it in 205,000 copies at $2.75 each of his 1938 bestseller "The Grapes of Wrath" and U.S. Steel had said a few years back it had no full-time workers. For the few who had any spare change, you could buy a Nash for $770 or the better Packard for $867-and-up or rent a five-room apartment in New York City complete with working fireplace for $135 a month. But the average industrial wage for those working was less than $1,400 a year.

With those kinds of problems, not even radio was going to get Americans riled up about somebody else's. It showed. The American Army was 19th in the world, just behind Portugal. In proportion to population, the United States was 45th. George Patton made colonel in 1938. He had family money, married more and had diverted his passion for polo into other steeds — tanks. He paid for spare parts for the few his unit had out of his own pocket.

That anyone stayed in the professional military is a testament to patriotism and probably lack of outside alternatives. Service involved dull routine in dusty, remote outposts punctuated with more exotic assignments and equally rare promotion. Dwight Eisenhower was a major for 16 years. Admittedly, he had postings to Paris and was aide to Chief of Staff Douglas MacArthur in Washington and again in the Philippines.

Omar Bradley, a 1915 West Point classmate of Eisenhower's, was like Ike a small-town Midwesterner waiting for luck or recognition to move him up the ladder. Happily, there was a pair of steady blue eyes that was watching. They belonged to George Catlett Marshall, second American in France in World War I where he excelled at staff work despite a prankish youth in Pennsylvania where he would douse his older sister's dates with water bombs. A graduate not of West Point but the Virginia Military Institute, he began keeping a "little black book" with the names of promising officers. As second in command at Fort Benning, Marshall expanded his notes, training such as Bradley, Mark Clark, Lucian Truscott, William Simpson, Courtney Hodges and Patton. ("He will take a unit through

"FLEET"

George Marshall was renowned as a trainer of men. But dogs?

He extravagantly loved his pet dalmatian "Fleet"whom everyone else considered stupid. Fleet, during the war, entered the K-9 Corps where he was cast in a training film. His role: the dog that couldn't do anything right.

hell and high water. But keep a tight rein around his neck.") Did he also list incompetents, Marshall was once asked. "There wouldn't have been room," he answered.

Marshall, highly recommended to Roosevelt by, among others, Gen. John J. Pershing, American commander in France in World War I, became Chief of Staff of the Army September 1, 1939, the day Germany invaded Poland. He was one of the few who knew what the radio news from abroad meant to his country. Now it was his firm persuasion to do something about it.

In 1939 the Army had the only semi-automatic infantry rifle in the world, the M-1 Garand. But only 8,000 were on hand. The artillery had but four 155 mm Long Tom cannons, 3,000 machine guns and as many French 75s, a cannon designed in 1897. Marshall told Congress the Army's 37 mm antitank gun was a good replacement for the .50-caliber machine gun as an anti-tank weapon. "But at present we have only one gun." The U.S. Army had 170,000 men in 1939 and its Air Corps 56 squadrons and 2,500 pilots. Boeing could make only 38 of its estimable B-17 Flying Fortresses a year.

Congress was scarcely any more bellicose. In 1935 it passed the Neutrality Law which prohibited U.S. ships from trading with any belligerent. It was revised to cover loans to belligerents and, acknowledging Spain, included civil wars. It passed 376-16 in the House and 63-6 in the Senate. After the U.S. gunboat Panay was sunk by Japanese bombers in China in December 1937, Rep. Leon Ludlow introduced a bill forbidding Congress to declare war until it had been approved by a national referendum. The bill didn't pass but got 209 votes. Clearly, the White House would have to talk very softly before it could carry a big stick.

Roosevelt was often a devious manipulator who liked to play one person off against another, smoothing it over with a jovial, first-name camaraderie. Early in Marshall's tenure, the President was chatting about arms policy in a meeting and turned to Marshall: "Don't you think so, George?" Maybe Mrs. Marshall called the soft-spoken but piercing-eyed general "George" but few others dared. "I'm sorry, Mr. President," Marshall replied, "but I don't agree with that at all."

Onlookers thought Marshall would soon be walking sentry duty at Arlington Cemetery. But Roosevelt said nothing. He just never called him George again.

By the end of 1940 the U.S. counted 170,000 soldiers, 109 squadrons and 4,000 pilots. Marshall had yet to find an army, but Roosevelt had found a general.

HITLER, U.S.A.

One of the most powerful voices on radio in the 1930s belonged to Father Charles E. Coughlin. His venomous sermons of hate and anti-Semitism reached a network audience that even outdrew "Amos & Andy." He was a pro-German, anti-Roosevelt, anti-war master at manipulating the new medium. He called Roosevelt's New Deal "Jew Deal," Roosevelt a "liar" who should be dealt with "by the use of bullets."

At a time when concentration camps were being barbwired across Hitler's Reich, Coughlin's sonorous voice boomed over the air: "When we get through with the Jews, they'll think the treatment they received in Germany was nothing."

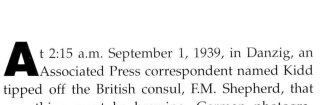

4

"WHITE"

1939

At 2:15 a.m. September 1, 1939, in Danzig, an Associated Press correspondent named Kidd tipped off the British consul, F.M. Shepherd, that something must be brewing. German photographers were winding new film into their cameras.

At 4:17 a.m. the old 1902 German battleship Schleswig-Holstein, purportedly in town on a ceremonial visit, opened fire on Polish defenses.

World War II had begun. German soldiers landed and rushed the Danzig post office, a strongpoint where the 51 Polish workers had firearms. They

Above: Jubilant Germans roll into Danzig in 1939, the spark that ignited World War II with the invasion of Poland.

Left: Poland was no match for Germany's blitzkrieg in 1939. Troops raise a frontier barrier to march into Danzig, Hitler's excuse for the invasion.

barricaded themselves in the basement. The Germans poured in gasoline and lit it. Four Poles escaped, 12 were killed. The rest were shot. In Beilitz near the Polish-Czech border, German troops herded the town's Jews into a synagogue and incinerated them. In Bydgoscz, 1,000 Jews were crammed into a barn and machine-gunned to death.

Hitler called the invasion of Poland "Case White." Again, it was a gamble. "I have met the umbrella men," the Fuhrer said. "The coffee sippers in London and Paris will stay this time, too. A world war will never, never, never come out of Case White." To mass his forces in Poland, Hitler had left his western front facing France with no tanks and enough cannon shells for only three days. But in one of the most astonishing moves in the annals of diplomacy, he had secured his eastern frontier. On August 23, Germany and Russia signed a nonaggression pact which stunned the world and left national communist parties actually speechless.

"CANNED GOODS"

Even Adolf Hitler was aware of the desirability of image. "Operation Canned Goods" was an elaborate scenario to turn the facts 180 degrees for German and world opinion.

Franz Koniok, a 40-year-old farm machinery salesman who thought the Poles were being unfairly bullied by Germany, was arrested by the Gestapo August 30, 1939. The next day he was shot and dressed in a Polish military uniform. At 8 p.m. a group of German soldiers also dressed as Poles stormed into the radio station in the German border town of Gleiwitz. Although the station was only a relay transmitter for a larger station in Breslau and only broadcast emergency weather, they seized the mike, fired a few shots over the air, cried "Long live Poland!" and departed, leaving behind Koniok's body as "proof" that Poland had attacked Germany.

Overnight, communism's most hated foe became its most powerful friend.

Britain and France had been romancing Moscow for months to no avail. On August 25, Britain finally drew the line by promising to fight if Poland were invaded. Geography left any direct intervention out of the question. But it meant war. On September 3, 1939, Britain and France made it official. Wehrmacht generals later admitted France could have reached Berlin with ease had its army come out from behind its Maginot Line. Instead, the French contented themselves on September 7 with an offensive by some of its 93 divisions on a limited 15-mile front. Driving pigs before them through minefields, the troops advanced a mile-and-a-half. One large unit was held up for a whole day by a single German machine gunner. Some of the Siegfried defenses were only wooden silhouettes but the French didn't advance far enough to find out.

Poland had the fifth largest army in the world. Thirty divisions faced 59 of Germany. But the Poles had no air power. Dashing cavalrymen charged German tanks with lances, being told the tanks were made of cardboard. German planes swept the skies, bombing Warsaw while Stukas terror-bombed Polish villages. While the blitzkrieg rolled on, some

German units had refused to attack. A third of the Wehrmacht had only a 14-day supply of ammunition.

Goering himself said: "If we lose the war, then God have mercy on us." The anti-Nazi German Chief of Staff, Gen. Franz Halder, talked of killing Hitler, but nothing came of it. Ernst von Weizacker, German Secretary of State, said: "There is nothing in my upbringing that would fit me to kill a man." He did not yet know his son had died in Poland.

Lloyd George had said that without Russia as an ally, Britain's guarantees to Poland meant nothing. Russia demonstrated as much September 17 by invading Poland from the east. A secret clause in the nonaggression treaty had already provided for Germany and Russia to divide up Poland. While rumors of war's imminence had been common, Poland was surprised by the German attack. This even though a handful of brilliant Polish mathematicians had built replicas of Germany's secret code machine, the Enigma. England, too, was taken unawares. In London, John Gielgud, Jack Hawkins and Peggy Ashcroft had been starring in Oscar Wilde's play, "The Importance of Being Earnest." Suddenly audiences, everybody, began carrying gas masks. Women were warned that wearing them caused mascara to run. Eton students were told they no longer had to wear top hats in order to fit the masks. Those issued to children were painted to resemble Mickey Mouse.

Chamberlain had declared war at noon. Within minutes, air raid sirens sounded. Radar, the new British invention, had picked up a blip. It actually was the plane of the French air attache returning from Paris. But two Hurricane fighters scrambled, collided and one pilot was killed, Britain's first casualty of World War II. In a demonstration of solidarity, Chamberlain made Churchill First Lord of the Admiralty, a job he held in the earlier war until he was sacked for the disastrous Gallipoli campaign. "Winston is back," the Admiralty cabled all hands.

The day Russia struck Poland, Germany's U-30 submarine sank the liner Athenia with a loss of 112 lives, including 28 Americans. The U.S. ambassador to London, Joseph P. Kennedy, sent his young son Jack to Scotland to handle the American survivors. The same day another U-boat sank the British carrier Courageous off the English coast. "Damn fine shot," said the skipper, Capt. W.T. Makeig-Jones, as he saluted the Royal Navy's white ensign and went down with his ship.

After the last Poles surrendered, Kennedy wired Roosevelt that the war was nearly over and Roosevelt should play the peacemaker. "The silliest message I ever received," said the President. Hitler, also playing peacemaker, told the Reichstag: "Germany has no further claims against France ... nowhere have I ever acted contrary to British interest."

In America, a Gallup poll showed only 2.5 percent of the people favored joining Britain and France. Thirty percent wanted nothing to do with any warring nation. But on November 4, 1939, Congress voted to repeal the Neutrality Act, authorized aid to the Allies on a cash-and-carry basis and outlined sea zones for American ships to stay out of.

Even before the shooting stopped, the Germans began shipping Jews by train to Lublin where they were corralled in a ghetto encircled by barbed wire. On December 27 of that fateful year, two German

KATYN

Sometime in 1940, possibly March, about 12,000 captured Polish officers were gathered in the Katyn forest outside Smolensk in eastern Russia, then murdered. Trees were planted over the mass grave which was unearthed by the Germans in 1943. Russia and Germany blamed each other for the massacre. Years later Russia admitted the deed. Asked at the time what to do with the prisoners, Stalin sent a one word order: "Liquidate."

soldiers were killed in a bar in the Warsaw suburb of Waver. The Germans hanged the owner outside the premises, then shot 120 men who happened to live in the area.

5

"YELLOW"

1940

Maj. Erich Honmann had some dirty laundry, missed his wife in Cologne and could have used some flying time. Therefore, when Maj. Helmut Reinberger asked for a lift to Cologne, Honmann was happy to start up his Me-108 and take off. Reinberger's briefcase contained Hitler's "Plan Yellow," the invasion of France, and Reinber-

Above: Hitler seemingly dances a jig— movies of the scene were actually doctored to indicate as much— after accepting France's surrender in the same railroad car at Compiegne where Germany surrendered in World War I.

Left: Germans inspect a plaque honoring Marshal Ferdinand Foch at the railroad car in Compiegne. The historic car was taken to Berlin where it was destroyed in an air raid.

ger was flying to a meeting to discuss it. Unfortunately, January 10, 1940, was foggy. Honmann got lost and crash-landed in Belgium. A peasant ran up. Reinberger asked him for a match and began burning his papers. Then soldiers arrived and put out the fire. They took the two Germans to headquarters where Reinberger threw Plan Yellow into a stove. A Belgian soldier pulled it out, badly burning his hands.

Adolf Hitler began reconsidering his now compromised Yellow.

As drawn, Yellow was to follow Germany's Schlieffen Plan that opened World War I: an attack through the Low Countries. One of the army's best brains, Field Marshal Erich von Manstein, had a better idea: attack through the forested Ardennes to the English Channel, trapping the Allied armies in Belgium. Hitler's famed intuition had been thinking the same. Yellow became Sichelschmitt (cut of the sickle).

31

Germany invaded Norway on short notice, fought off British landing attempts, but eventually fell into a trap when their large garrison there lay idle when urgently needed in Russia and Normandy.

Churchill was debating landing British troops in Norway, but Hitler struck first. German troops landed in Oslo in 1940 while the government was still mailing out mobilization notices.

"WESER" 1939

Scandinavia hoped to ride out the storm of World War II as it had the first, in neutrality. It was not to be.

After making severe territorial demands on Finland, Russian bombers attacked Helsinki November 30, 1939. Then came the Red Army. Finns recalled their national epic, The Kalevala: "Let our contests be in the winter/Let our wars be in the snowfields." In temperatures down to minus-50 degrees, their white clad, ski-equipped troops fought off the Russians heroically. The state liquor board supplied 70,000 bottles which were filled with gasoline, and the Molotov cocktail was born. Perhaps a million Russians died in mass attacks, their frozen bodies "stacked like firewood waiting to be chopped." Finnish President Kyosti Kellio was finally forced to sign a cease-fire March 12, 1940, saying, "Let the hand wither that is forced to sign such a paper." A few months later a stroke crippled his hand.

*   *   *   *

Germany depended on iron ore from Sweden's mines inland from the northern Norwegian port of Narvik. Churchill had planned to seize the mines but Hitler struck first. On February 21, 1940, he gave Lt. Gen. Nikolaus von Falkenhurst four hours to draft an invasion plan. Furiously consulting a Baedeker travel guide, Falkenhurst did so: "Operation Weser."

On April 9, under the very nose of the Royal Navy which had been tipped off but sortied the wrong way, German troops overran Denmark in four hours and landed in Norway by sea and air. Oslo was still putting mobilization orders in the mail as German transports landed at the city airport. Britain landed troops at Trondheim and Narvik in makeshift efforts. The Trondheim force's mortar ammunition was left behind. Field phones went to Trondheim, their cables to Narvik. Britain evacuated its last 25,000 soldiers from Narvik June 6-7 — something they were becoming adept at — with the loss of two destroyers and the carrier Glorious. Hitler had his iron as well as North Atlantic submarine bases, but Weser cost him three of Germany's eight cruisers and 10 of 20 destroyers, a severe loss to a possible invasion of Britain.

The Ardennes woods were dense. Henri Petain, France's savior at Verdun in 1917, called them "impenetrable." But in 1938 Gen. Alphonse George had led seven French divisions through the Ardennes in war games and warned Germany could do likewise. Gen. Maurice Gustave Gamelin, the aged French commander, hushed up George's report. Instead, he planned to rush troops and armor into Belgium once Germany struck. The Ardennes would be lightly defended by second tier divisions and French colonials from Morocco and Madagascar. Leaders of the British Expeditionary Force objected. They had built 400 pillboxes, 100 miles of railroad track and 59 airstrips along the Belgian border. Some 400,000 British soldiers had dug in, even planted their own vegetable gardens. Nonetheless, in February 1940, BEF commander Lord Gort yielded to Gamelin.

The so-called Phoney War or Sitzkrieg had kept the western front quiet all winter. Hitler and weather had postponed Yellow several times. Halder and Gen. Walther von Brauchitsch, Hitler's army commanders, had even been plotting to eliminate the Fuhrer until he chewed out the cowering von Brauchitsch in a towering rage.

Things were so dull, alcoholism was becoming a problem among the bored, entombed Maginot troops. French pay was as low as morale. Some soldiers moonlighted as taxi drivers. For the officers, their biggest question seemed at times to be if the Grand Marnier souffle would rise. French Gen. Charles Huntziger set his shivering colonials to work clearing tank traps out of the Ardennes so his cavalry could maneuver. It seemed not to have occurred to him that tanks might come the other way.

The Allies had 136 divisions on line, same as the Germans who had fewer tanks — 2,400 to 3,000 — but more planes — 3,000 to 1,800. Three-quarters of the French tanks, however, had no radios. They were also encumbered by a strategy of dissipating their massed strength by dispersing them among their infantry divisions, much to the disgust of Col. Charles de Gaulle, a tanker and unheeded apostle of Liddell Hart's lightning war theories.

On April 30, the French military attache in Berne passed on intelligence that Germany would strike May 8 or 10 with the "center of gravity" on Sedan on the Meuse River, gateway to the Ardennes. French pilots reported the tanks of the seven panzer

WINSTON

On May 7, Leo Amery rose in Parliament and assaulted Chamberlain with the famous denunciation of the Long Parliament by Oliver Cromwell: "You have sat too long here for any good you have been doing. Depart, I say, and let us have done with you. In the name of God, go!"

King George VI would have preferred Lord Halifax replace Chamberlain, but Halifax declined. In early afternoon May 10, Chamberlain resigned in favor of Churchill. Three days later Britain's new prime minister declared to the House of Commons: "I have nothing to offer you but blood, toil, tears and sweat...You ask what is our aim? I can answer in one word: victory!"

divisions backed up 75 miles aimed at the "impenetrable" forest. Gamelin stood pat. At dawn May 10 the real war began. As a decoy Gen. Gerd von Rundstedt attacked through Holland and Belgium to make the Allies think Yellow was still in effect. German gliders landed on the top of Eben Emael fortress, the "impregnable" bastion of Belgian defenses. With grenades and flamethrowers aimed through the cannon slits, they captured the fort in 24 hours. At the Maas River bridge in Gennep, Holland, soldiers dressed as Dutch policemen crossed over from the German side with a "prisoner" with his hands up. Dutch border guards opened the gates for the regular morning train from Germany. It was filled with German troops who with the fake policemen quickly secured the crossing. Rotterdam was bombed to ruin as Sichelscmitt worked to perfection. Except for the officer who had packed his dress uniform to accept surrender of the neutral Netherlands from Queen Wilhelmina. She fled to England.

Hans Oster, Chief of Staff of the Abwehr, Germany's intelligence agency, was a vehement closet anti-Nazi. He told Gisbertus Sas, the Dutch military attache in Berlin, before the attack to "burn the Meuse bridges for me." Hitler's opposition in Germany had even warned the Vatican. But by May 14, the panzers of tank genius Heinz Guderian had three bridgeheads across the Meuse. The French army east of Sedan pivoted counterclockwise to protect the rear of the Maginot Line. This opened a

62-mile gap, and Guderian's tanks poured through. To his north the 7th Panzer Division, its commanding general in the lead tank urging his men on like a jockey, also crossed the Meuse. This was Gen. Erwin Rommel, who had never even been in a tank until his recent appointment to the armored. Lacking a patron of influence, he had languished in the military until, as head of Hitler's bodyguard, he landed the biggest patron of all. Across the Meuse, Rommel raced 50 miles overnight.

The BEF moved as planned into Belgium to find its promised defenses only half-built. One Belgian border guard even refused to let a British unit cross. Someone gave J.L. Hidson some tulips. He wrote of the flowers in his diary: "Take a long look at me and enjoy me while you can. Who knows how long it will be?" The French in Belgium fought off the Germans for a time, but lost 100 tanks to the unopposed Stukas and fell back. By May 17, Guderian was halfway to the Channel, speeding across old World War I battlefields where millions had died in a stalemate of meters. Hitler, suddenly cautious, ordered Guderian to stop to let the rest of the army catch up. Furious, Guderian persuaded headquarters to permit him a "reconnaissance in force." He laid phone lines from his tanks so the OKW couldn't intercept his radio messages, then took off. He made 200 miles in 10 days. On May 20, the British Post Office announced a "serious technical failure" on the London-Paris service. "We have no idea when service will be restored."

In Paris, where only days before shoppers on the tony Rue de Rivoli had been buying curios in china of a terrier lifting its leg on a copy of "Mein Kampf," panic took over. On May 15, Prime Minister Paul Reynaud phoned Churchill to say: "We have been defeated. We have lost the battle." Churchill flew to Paris two days later to buck him up. "Where is the strategic reserve?" he asked in the schoolboy French he took unjustified pride in. "Aucune," he was told. There is none.

The French pleaded for more British fighters. Antoine de St. Exupery, flier and writer, said the French air force had disappeared "as if you dashed glassfuls of water into a forest fire."

Gen. Hugh Dowding, head of Britain's Fighter Command, protested so violently to Churchill that onlookers were afraid he might shoot him. If Britain kept feeding its Hurricanes and Spitfires into the

---

MEANWHILE

Sobered by the rout in France, Roosevelt in May asked Congress to authorize plans to produce 50,000 planes a year and a two-ocean navy.

When told, Goering scoffed: "You need a psychiatrist to examine your head. America can make cars and refrigerators but not aircraft."

By the end of the war the Allies, principally the United States, built 400,248 more planes than Germany.

French inferno, it would have none left within 10 days. It would mean "the final, complete and irremedial defeat of our country." Throughout the entire preceding winter, France had manufactured only 60 planes a month. And no tanks at all. Churchill compromised: British planes would fly but only from English bases.

On May 21, Gort temporarily stopped Rommel with an attack by one brigade and 74 tanks. He would have had more, but French Gen. Rene Altmayer wouldn't join in and merely "wept silently in his bed." With no anti-tank cannons, Gort's men threw china plates at the panzers. When the commanders popped out of their turrets at the unwarlike noise, snipers shot them.

Roads everywhere were jammed with refugees: in Citroens and Panhards, in farm carts, bicycles, even a girl on roller skates. "An immense human carpet," said a survivor, "with mattresses on car roofs to protect from the Stukas." Hans Habe, a Hungarian novelist serving in the French army, joined "limping soldiers trying in vain to walk like soldiers in the presence of fleeing women ... the disordered funeral procession of a disorganized army." Farmers refused food to the refugees and pleaded with them to go elsewhere lest they attract the Stukas.

"How is it possible these French soldiers ... would allow themselves to go more or less voluntarily into imprisonment?" a German soldier wondered. "They did not (even) keep their heads up."

As Guderian reached the Channel cutting off the BEF and French in Belgium, which surrendered May 28, Hitler made an unannounced visit to the panzers' headquarters in Charleville. Aides hur-

ASTROLOGY

On November 8, 1939, Hitler returned to the Munich beer hall for the 16th anniversary of his putsch. An astrologer predicted an assassination attempt, but aides chose not to tell the Fuhrer. Sure enough, George Elser, a communist sympathizer recently released from Dachau, had carefully wired a bomb where Hitler would speak. It was timed to explode at 11:20 p.m. However, the usually long-winded dictator finished his harangue early and left abruptly at 11:07. The bomb exploded on time, killing seven and injuring 63 including the father of Eva Braun, Hitler's constant companion.

riedly waved cigarette smoke out the windows and hid the schnapps bottles in a file cabinet. Guderian's tanks were only 12 miles from Dunkirk when the Fuhrer made one of his greatest mistakes of the war. He ordered Guderian to stop.

6

"DYNAMO"

1940

Considering that he had been second officer of the Titanic, that he was happily raising chickens in Hertfordshire, one could understand if Charles Herbert Lightoller had had it with the sea. On the contrary, he delighted in cruising on the Thames aboard his 58-foot motor yacht Sundowner. One trip he'd taken 21 guests. So when the call went out, the 66-year-old Lightoller took his son, Roger, and a

The two-way railroad car, above, where the Allies accepted Germany's surrender in 1918 and Hitler dictated armistice to France 22 years later. At left, Hitler at the Compiegne capitulation with his generals, the servile Wilhelm Keitel, left, who was hanged at war's end, and Walther von Brauchitsch who eventually quit.

deck hand and cast off for a second encounter with history.

Sundowner joined one of the most romantic, motley and brave flotillas that ever put to sea, more than 800 vessels of all kinds. Almost all segments of a seafaring nation set off from Ramsgate, Margate, Dover and other ports across the Channel to rescue the trapped BEF at Dunkirk. There were destroyers and ferries and paddle wheelers and 28-foot cockle-fishing boats and lifeboats and Thames sailing barges and family runabouts and yachting "gin palaces" and ocean racers and mine sweepers and trawlers and schuitjes — powered canal barges escaped from Holland that the British simplified to "skoots." Recreational sailors from London's financial City answered the call still wearing striped pants. The Royal Ocean Yacht Club was deserted except for the doorman. From fisherman to career Navy to an American theater director who'd been studying navigation for fun, they all had to contend

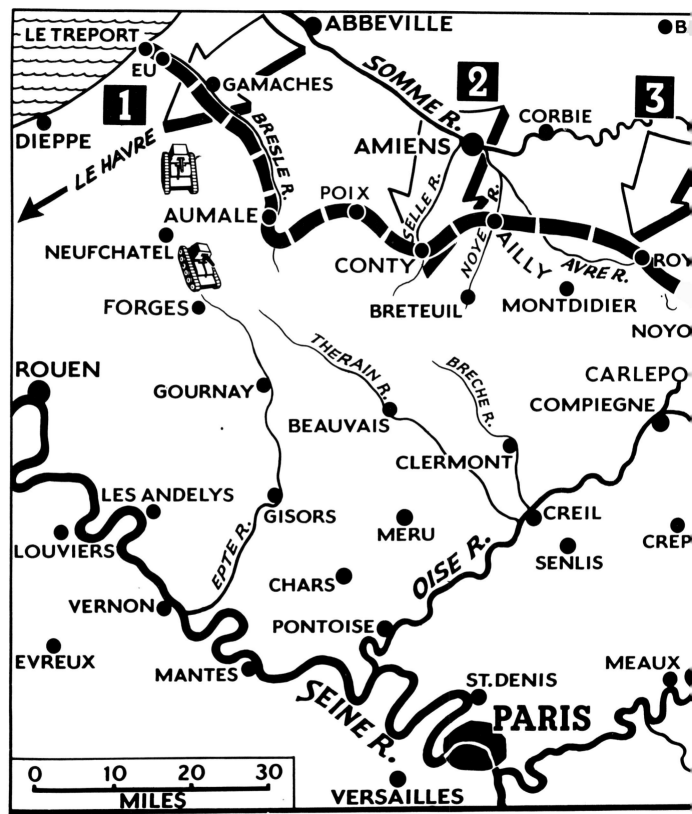

German forces set up for their drive south through France.

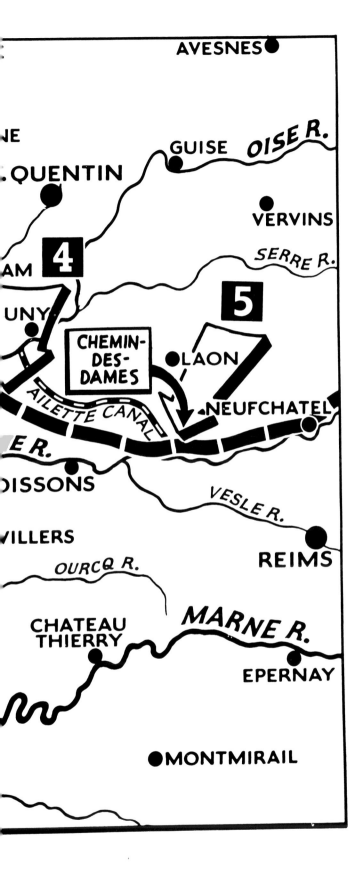

BALTICS

Not to be outdone by Germany, Russia in June 1940 took over the Baltic states of Estonia, Latvia and Lithuania and forced Bessarabia from Romania.

with strafing and bombing, fog, a 2.6-knot current, 19-foot tides on the beach and the wartime absence of buoys. And death.

The lift began May 27. It was directed by Vice Adm. Sir Bertram Ramsay from a concrete room in an old Dover power plant, hence the name, Operation Dynamo. Hitler also played a part.

Why he let the BEF get away is debated still. Goering, whose Luftwaffe was a creation of the Nazis and was judged more loyal than the Prussian-dominated OKW, lobbied the Fuhrer to let his planes finish off the encircled Allies. A more cogent explanation is that von Rundstedt, more cautious than the younger, tank-minded Guderian, feared an attack from French armies to the south to liberate the pocket. Also, much of the panzers needed maintenance. Another reason? Gen. Guenther von Blumentritt was with Hitler during the fateful three days he had put the brakes on Guderian. Later he recalled Hitler "compared the British Empire with the Catholic Church, saying they were both essential elements of the stability of the world." This sounds un-Hitlerian, but the Fuhrer was a secret admirer of the British whose customary common sense, he sometimes thought, had deserted them for a foolish determination to press on in a losing battle. This argument weakens, though, considering the all-out attacks by the Luftwaffe on Dunkirk.

The three-day respite did, however, permit the

ORAN

To keep the French fleet from falling into German hands, the Royal Navy destroyed a large part of it in an attack July 3, 1940, at the naval base at Mers-el-Kebir outside Oran, killing 1,297 sailors. The raid further embittered Anglo-French relations.

> On January 14, 1941, a refugee Belgian politician, Victor de Lavelye, broadcast over the BBC that "V for Victory" — in Morse code three dots and a dash — should be the rallying symbol of occupied Europe. The opening notes of Beethoven's Fifth Symphony, which had the same cadence, became an anthem of resistance.

BEF and the French to put up a perimeter defense. The pleasurable Channel sands became hell. Mutilated bodies — soldiers, a woman still clutching her purse, bloated horses — washed to and fro at the tide line. Terrified dogs chewed at them. Tommies drunk on looted wine fed some to horses who bolted crazily among the bomb blasts. Wounded soldiers were trundled on wheelbarrows onto makeshift piers of sunken lorries. Boat decks were so crowded with standees the mortally wounded remained upright when they died. Some soldiers waited patiently in endless queues, others fought their way onto beached small craft, capsizing their would-be rescuers despite gunfire from their skippers. A bomb blew the bow off the destroyer Montrose. Two tugs towed it, stern first. Two soldiers paddled away in a canoe. Pvt. Bill Hersey dressed his French war bride in battle gear and took her along. Soldiers lay on their backs firing their Enfield rifles at the Stukas. Overhead RAF fighters, grounded often by bad weather, attacked, the Germans recalled, "with the fury of maniacs" although Tommies on the ground raged bitterly at the lack of air cover. The two moles flanking the entrance to Dunkirk harbor crawled with humanity like crabs at high tide. A bomb dropped down a funnel of destroyer Grenade blowing a midshipman into the sea. His entire report of the incident read: "There was a bloody great bang. I have the honor to be your obedient servant." Some returning crews refused to go back to Dunkirk's carnage.

On the perimeter, the Allies fell back grudgingly. One officer was told by his commander not to withdraw beyond a certain tree. When he did anyway, the commander ordered two riflemen to shoot him. He dropped.

On the biggest day, June 1, the flotilla took off 68,000 men. Early on, most of the evacuees were British. Sensitive already to charges by the French of abandonment, particularly the husbanding of its fighter squadrons, the British began taking off more Frenchmen. Some of the French fishermen took their countrymen down the coast to Cherbourg so they could fight again.

The Lightollers carefully piled soldiers into Sundowner, instructing them to lie prone so the yacht wouldn't become top heavy. First the cabins filled up, then the decks. When Sundowner got back to England, the men poured ashore like clowns from a tiny auto. Sundowner brought home 130 men.

All told 338,226 soldiers — and 170 dogs — were brought off at Dunkirk, a third of them French. The last day was June 4. From Dover, Adm. Ramsay could read through binoculars the time on the clock tower in Calais across the Channel. It was now occupied France.

When the last 30,000 soldiers holding the perimeter were overrun, a German general asked their commander where the BEF was. "Gone" was the reply. "Gone back to England."

* * * *

France's agony was soon over. On June 10, Mussolini declared war to join in the spoils. Fearful of alienating the Italian-American vote, Roosevelt put in, took out, then put back in a famous phrase in a speech: "The hand that held the dagger has stuck it into the back of his neighbor." But the lust for battle in France, never strong, had gone. The British wanted to use an airfield in Marseille to bomb Italy. The French blocked the runway. The Italians might retaliate.

On June 14, Hitler's legions goosestepped under the Arc de Triomphe as U.S. Ambassador William Bullitt surrendered Paris in the absence of the fled government. German MPs directed traffic as the gendarmes looked on.

In a last-ditch effort to bolster the demoralized French, Churchill on June 6 ordered the 52nd Lowland Division and the 1st Canadian Division, two of the last fully manned fighting units left in Britain, to France. Rommel, meanwhile, was racing along the Channel coast towards Normandy. He trapped the British 51st Division in the port of St. Valery. Only 3,300 French and English troops could be evacuated.

Rommel dashed ahead, covering 150 miles on June 17, the one-day record for the war. Allied hopes to set up a redoubt in Brittany came to naught. De Gaulle flew from Brittany to England, arriving with four shirts, two pairs of pants and a portrait of his family. He quickly set up the Council for the Defense of the Empire, which became known as the Free French, based in Brazzaville, French Congo.

With Rommel right on their heels, the two divisions Churchill had just sent to France were successfully evacuated from Cherbourg with almost all of their equipment. All told, 160,000 Allied soldiers got away in a far more successful, if unheralded, evacuation than Dunkirk.

On June 21, France formally surrendered to Hitler in the same raiload car at Compiegne where 22 years earlier the roles had been reversed. Versailles had been avenged. Hitler shipped the car to Berlin where it was later destroyed in an air raid. He also installed the Louvre's Winged Victory of Samothrace in his office. He painted a picture of it for his Christmas cards. Subsequently, mattresses and stoves were removed from the Maginot Line to equip air raid shelters in Berlin. Orchards were planted among the fortifications.

The old marshal, Petain, became head of unoccupied France, run from the spa town of Vichy. He replaced Bastille Day, July 14, with May Day as the national holiday. Jews were to be restricted to no more than 2 percent of jobs in the professions, 3 percent of students. Jewish property began to be confiscated. But Parisian women were already being marked down for future judgment for "horizontal collaboration" with the Germans. The highly organized Communist Party began forming an underground. The German commander in Nantes was murdered. Ninety-eight Frenchmen were executed for it. Yellow was done but not the war.

7

"SEA LION"

1940

In the early days of radio, British stations noted a curiosity: sometimes their broadcasts went on the fritz when planes flew near transmitters. In an island ever sensitive to the threat of hostile technology, this phenomenon in time came to the attention of a scientific advisory panel of the Air Ministry. Perchance a death ray of some sort might be devised to shoot invasive planes from the sky.

In 1935, Robert Watson-Watt, a Scot who headed the Radio Research branch of the National Physical Laboratory, had a more down-to-earth idea. If not destroying planes, maybe radio waves could at least

Above: *A picture taken from the nose of a German plane captures a British pilot bailing out from his crippled Hurricane fighter during the Battle of Britain.*

Left: *St. Paul's Cathedral still stood after the German blitz bombing of London, a symbol of British survival.*

detect them. Indeed. By the outbreak of war, 20 towering transmitters girded the English coast from Newcastle around to Southampton. Radar.

This was not the only scientific contribution that in 1940 was about to save Britain and the free world it alone now represented. In 1919, a Dutchman named Hugo Koch had invented a coding machine he thought might be useful to close-mouthed industrialists. He called the device Enigma after British composer Sir Edward Elgar's "Enigma Variations," a musical cipher. By pairing electrically-driven rotors and a keyboard in no more space than an overweight typewriter, Koch had a machine that could produce variations to the number 150 followed by 18 zeroes. Germany quickly snapped up Enigma as the basis for their military codes. A handful of brilliant Polish codebreakers duplicated the machine. So did the French with the aid of a German turncoat and a French-American cash register firm. On August 8, 1939, the French delivered

A German Messerschmitt zeroes in on a Spitfire in the summer skies of 1940 over England. But it was the RAF which prevailed in the Battle of Britain, convincing Hitler not to invade.

by hand an Enigma to the British at Victoria station. The Poles also turned over their information. But a barrier remained: how to decipher the keys for Enigma, which changed daily.

In 1936 Beryl Power, a one-time British suffragette, began compiling a list of the best brains in the United Kingdom. By the start of the war it contained 80,000 names. One belonged to Alan Mathison Turing, born in 1912 to an intellectual mother and a father in the Indian civil service. Turing was brilliant, eccentric and, eventually, a tragic suicide. After a Ph.D. at Cambridge, he studied with Albert Einstein at the Institute for Advanced Study in Princeton, New Jersey. The war begun, Turing was assigned to a bizarre assemblage of codebreakers at Bletchley Park, an old Victorian estate 40 miles north

of London. Said Churchill of the group: "I told you to leave no stone unturned in your recruiting. I did not expect you to take me so literally." Even among that extraordinary cast, Turing stood out. He wore a gas mask for hay fever, would jog to London timing himself with an alarm clock tied to his wrist and kept a long distance phone line open during BBC broadcasts of "Larry the Lamb" to discuss the child's play with his mother. But in May, as France was falling, Turing and his team perfected a machine that was a clicking and clattering ancestor of the computer and could read radio intercepts of Enigma messages. The decipherments were called Ultra, the name of the code Britain used at Trafalgar.

With Ultra, Britain could know the Germans were coming. With radar it could see them.

On July 2, 1940, Hitler decided upon Sea Lion, the invasion of Britain, the first since the Normans of 1066. But he hedged: "... A landing is possible provided that air supremacy can be attained..." Historian Peter Fleming, brother of Ian who created James Bond, in his book on Sea Lion is another who comments on Hitler's ambivalence toward Britain: "He alternately wanted them on his side and at his feet."

Winston Churchill possessed no such ambiguities. Knowing what was coming, he said in one of his most famous speeches June 18: "Let us therefore ... so bear ourselves that if the British Empire and the Commonwealth last 1,000 years, men will say 'This was their finest hour.'"

There were in the entire kingdom only 22 divisions, only half of them anywhere near battle ready. A million over- and under-aged men volunteered for the Home Guard. They brought shotguns and fowling pieces and old family swords off manorial walls, even golf clubs. Four dozen rifles were found in the prop room of the Drury Lane Theater. If all else failed, the chaps were advised to throw pepper in the invaders' eyes. The Queen took pistol practice in the garden at Buckingham Palace, vowing not to be taken without a fight.

All road and railway station signs were removed. Barricades blocked golf fairways against air landings. Church bells were only to be rung in case of invasion. A vicar went to jail for a sabbath violation. Motorists were required to remove the distributor rotors of their cars when not in use, lest the enemy drive off in them. All binoculars and aluminum pans were turned in. Kite flying was forbidden for "other than servants of His Majesty." London zookeepers were issued rifles to kill the inhabitants if bombs ruptured their enclosures. The poisonous snakes and scorpions were killed. To save manpower, juries were reduced from 12 to seven members. BBC announcers for the first time identified themselves on the air to guard against saboteurial messages. Not everything changed. The Times dutifully reported that a great crested grebe had been spotted in an air raid shelter in Euston.

Britain's position as a last bastion was illustrated by London hotel guest lists. King Zog, whose Albania had been invaded by Italy in 1939, was at the Ritz. Queen Wilhelmina and later King George of Greece were at the Claridge. King Haakon of Norway put up at his embassy.

The Battle of Britain proper began July 10, 1940. "I think we have managed to avoid losing the war," diarist and government official Harold Nicholson wrote his wife. "But when I think how on earth we are going to win it, my imagination quails."

The RAF had had an unsung hero in charge of Fighter Command since 1936. He was future Air Marshal Sir Hugh Dowding. He single-mindedly shepherded the design and production of the all-metal Hurricane fighter and the Spitfire, both a match for Germany's Me-109 and superior to the twin-engine Me-110. Powered by a Rolls-Royce Merlin engine, superior to anything Germany produced, they were death on the slow Stukas. On July 1 the RAF had 591 fighters, Germany 725.

Flying for the RAF were the legless Douglas Bader, Poles, Canadians, Australians, New Zealanders. Three American soldiers of fortune who had flown for Finland met an RAF commander in a pub and were sworn in the next day. Of eight Yanks in the battle, only one survived the war. There was 4-foot-10-inch "Shorty" Keogh raised to combat height in his cockpit by cushions. Entering August, the RAF had 1,434 fighter pilots, a month later but 840.

Daily the Luftwaffe came over and daily the RAF rose to defend their aerodromes and the radar towers that guided them. It was a war of attrition visible from the ground in contrail arabesques swirling and twisting across the summer sky. Squadron Leader Henry Hogan was shot down four times. Once his pickup found him seated in an armchair by his wreck, downing beer from a neighboring pub along with a plate of sandwiches. A pilot remembered a call from his mother: "I'm very worried about you, darling." "As I'd had several bullets fired at me during the day, I too, had been a trifle worried." "I don't think your batman is drying your socks properly. You might catch a nasty cold."

Alerted by Ultra and radar, ground control centers directed the battle. WAAFs in bunkers with croupier sticks moved little markers across charts, all the while monitoring the grim reality from the fighters' radios on high. One WAAF remembered a German pilot, a voice spiralling to death. "He screamed and screamed for his mother and cursed the Fuhrer the whole way down. I went out and was sick."

In August, the continued attacks on the air bases were killing off the more experienced fliers. That month, the Germans destroyed more fighters than Britain could make. Fighter Command lost 338 planes that month, the Luftwaffe 137 Me-109s. Then, on August 25, the Luftwaffe bombed London for the first time. Bomber Command immediately hit Berlin back. William Shirer noted in his diary: "The Berlin-

A composite photo shows the panorama of the destruction wrought by German bombers in the blitz of London in 1940-1.

GREECE

Without telling his Axis partner, on October 28, 1940, Mussolini invaded northern Greece. Hitler was furious, and so, soon, was Il Duce. His men, still wearing summer uniforms, were fought to a standstill in the snow by the Greeks who killed 20,000 Italians. A disgusted Mussolini said he might reforest the Appenines to bring snow and toughen his people, "our good-for-nothing Italians, this mediocre race ... Even Michelangelo had need of marble to make statues. If he had had only clay, he would have been nothing more that a potter."

ers are stunned. They did not think it could ever happen. Goering assured them that it couldn't."

The RAF was not beaten but attrition was taking a worrisome toll. Dowding had thrown in his reserves. Then on September 6, Hitler made another fateful decision. He switched the Luftwaffe from its promising campaign against the fighter bases to all-out bombing of London. His reasons appear to have been: 1 — revenge for the bombing of Berlin; 2 — to get the RAF to commit all its fighters and, 3 — to pound Britain into negotiation. He postponed Sea Lion to await the results.

The London Blitz brought out the best in the British. (And, infrequently, the worst. Looters some-times moved in before the dust had hardly settled. Ghouls stripped the dead of jewelry.) The city took to backyard bomb shelters and, by the millions, to the Underground where there were special sections for snorers. London became a cauldron of fire, smoke and rubble. The East End docks and their Cockney neighborhoods were devastated. But the ruin was met by a grim, monosyllabic stoicism. One housewife told a friend her 92-year-old father had been blown out of bed and his false teeth broken by a near hit. "Blimey!" was the only reply.

A bomb exploded in Buckingham Palace 80 yards from where King George sat. "Now we can look the East Enders in the eye," said the Queen. In his club,

St. Paul's Cathedral, right, and the Old Bailey, left, stand out as unyielding landmarks against a fiery background of the London blitz.

H.G. Wells refused to take shelter until served his cheese course. "Why should I be disturbed by some wretched little barbarian in a machine?" Golfers in the suburbs adjusted: "Players may take cover during air raids without penalty," said revised rules. The Buccaneers' cricket team had a 127-run lead blown away by an air raid.

Bad as the blitz was, it would have been worse had Hitler built heavy bombers and the long-range fighters to accompany them. He also misjudged the fortitude of the British people in "their finest hour." And he misjudged the RAF. Always the Hurricanes and Spitfires were there, rising to do battle. On September 15, what was to become celebrated as Battle of Britain Day, the RAF shot down 60 German aircraft, losing but 26.

Sea Lion had predicated staged landings on England's southeast coast. But the RAF had not been defeated. Nor had the Royal Navy, the world's strongest despite some severe body blows. Bomber Command repeatedly struck massed German landing barges in the Channel invasion ports. Hitler postponed Sea Lion. He had gambled on yet another

HESS

The same night of London's last major raid, Rudolf Hess titular No. 3 in the Third Reich hierarchy because of past loyalties but far lower in the pecking order because of limited acuity, hopped into an Me-110 and amazed the world by flying to Scotland. He wanted to parachute in on the Duke of Hamilton, the first man to fly over Everest and whom Hess had been impressed by at the 1936 Olympics.

Hess, a veteran World War I pilot, flipped the plane and fell out. On landing he was met by a farmer with a pitchfork who called authorities. While waiting, the farmer's wife offered the Deputy Reichsfuhrer some tea. "I never drink tea this late," he replied. Much conjecture has been made of Hess's purpose, but one was to convince Britain to make peace before Hitler opened a two-front war with the Soviet Union. Hess spent the rest of his life in prison, dying in 1987.

blitzkrieg and lost. He had been gaining an edge in the air battle of attrition, then changed tactics. And always there were the fighters with their red, white and blue bullseye emblems.

"Never," said Churchill in another line for the ages, "was so much owed by so many to so few." ("And for so little," cracked an RAF pilot who felt underpaid.)

Despite pillaging the conquered lands of Europe of resources and impressing slave labor, Germany was outproduced in planes by a submarine-besieged Britain in 1940-41, 35,000 to 23,500. From September 1940, Germany's plane output even de-clined sharply. Tantalizing as the green downs of England were just across the Channel, Hitler never quite summoned the nerve to leap. He would try something else. The last major raid of the blitz came on May 10, 1941. Westminster Abbey was badly damaged. Among the ancient, toppled stones lay a Book of Common Prayer. Ironically, its pages were open to: "... They have set fire upon the holy places."

By then, Britain had won the battle fought in its name. Hitler was not to officially abandon Sea Lion until February 13, 1942. By then anyone other than a fanatic such as himself would have realized his was a losing battle.

8

"DOG"

1940

Despite the fall of France and Britain's perilous agony, the United States in 1940 was like a slumberer between the morning alarm and feet on the floor.

Shirley Temple signed with MGM for $2,500 a week. "For Whom the Bell Tolls," Ernest Hemingway's novel of the Spanish Civil War, was the best seller. It sold "like frozen daiquiris in hell," the author gloated. Duke Ellington wrote "Sophisticated Lady." Other ballads of the year were "The Way You Look Tonight," "Where or When," George Gershwin's "Summertime."

Franklin D. Roosevelt, running for an unprecedented third term against a Republican newcomer,

Roosevelt signs America's first peace time draft in 1940 as War Secretary Henry Stimson, left, and Army Chief of Staff Gen. George C. Marshall, second from right, look on.

51

Wendell Willkie, assured Americans: "I shall say it again and again and again: your boys are not going to be sent into any foreign wars." Charles A. Lindbergh, still America's hero, had seen Hilter's Luftwaffe first-hand, had even received an unexpected medal from Goering, and was impressed. He urged the United States to cooperate with Hitler if he won the war.

At Yale, a student named R. Douglas Stuart Jr., son of a vice president of Quaker Oats, formed an organization called America First. He enlisted such names as Gen. Robert E. Wood, president of Sears Roebuck, author Kathleen Norris, ad man Chester Bowles and Alice Roosevelt Longworth, TR's outspoken daughter. Within a year America First had 800,000 members in 400 chapters.

But there were other voices. Refugee physicists from Europe, one of Hitler's greatest contributions to Allied victory, warned of the awesome military potential of the atom. A recent graduate of the University of North Carolina, Ramsey Potts who would one day fly a bomber over a Romanian city called Ploesti, had seen Germany first-hand and it concerned him deeply.

George Marshall minced no words with Roosevelt, lecturing him: "If you don't do something and do it right away, I don't know what's going to happen to this country."

Marshall was torn by the tyranny of time. "Yesterday we had time but no money. Today we have money but no time." In the Army's maneuvers that fall, there were only four actual tanks. Allerton Cushman, a Wall Street investment banker and reserve lieutenant in the Field Artillery, recalled one page in the thick manual devoted to firing at moving targets. Leading them depended on whether they were at "the walk, the trot or the gallop." Horses!

Roosevelt had managed to squeeze America's first peacetime draft through Congress. On October 16, 1940, a blindfolded Henry Stimson, Secretary of War, reached into a goldfish bowl containing numbers 1 through 7,836 and drew out No. 158. The Army was taking 1 million men between ages 21 and 35. Only 36 refused to register. FDR stipulated the draftees would serve only in U.S. territory.

Bare as the military's cupboard was, there was never a lack of paper for plans. In late 1940, Adm. Harold "Betty" Stark was assigned to prepare revised contingency plans for war. (The robust, white-

JEEP

At a cocktail party in early 1940, then-War Secretary Harry Woodring was confronted by a salesman for the Bantam Motor Car Co. which manufactured in the States the equivalent of Britain's diminutive Austin. He had a proposal for a small all-purpose vehicle for the Army. Maj. Walter Bedell Smith was directed to look into it. Smith reported back to Marshall, breaking in on a meeting which Marshall sanctioned if the intruder could justify it.

"What do you think?" asked Marshall. "Good," Smith answered. "Then we'll do it," said Marshall. The first order was for 72 General Purpose vehicles, GPs, which in no time was de-bureaucratized to jeep.

haired 59-year-old sea dog got his belying nickname from his Annapolis plebe days when upperclassmen harassed him by requiring him to recite John Stark's Revolutionary War battle cry to his men: "Win today or Betty Stark will be a widow.") He alphabetized the alternative plans, the fourth being "D for Dog."

"Our entry into the war now seems to be WHEN and not WHETHER," he wrote (his emphasis). Should Britain be defeated, the United States "might not lose everywhere, but we might possibly not win anywhere."

Plan Dog, accordingly, promised that the first priority of the United States would be victory in Europe with a holding action against Japan in the Pacific. Plan Dog was further canonized by conversations between British and American chiefs of staff in Washington from January 29 to March 29, 1941.

Having defeated Willkie in November, Roosevelt was freer to nudge his reluctant nation. Britain was gradually going broke buying arms in the United States. Roosevelt was too canny to propose outright gifts to Britain. Instead he put it in terms to appeal to Yankee thrift: Lend-Lease. It was as if, said the President, you loaned a neighbor a hose to put out a fire. You didn't want money, just return of the hose.

In a fireside chat December 29, 1940, with a pack of Camels by the mike and Hollywood guests Clark Gable and Carole Lombard looking on, Roosevelt called on the nation to become "the arsenal of democracy."

An equally politic Churchill replied: "Give us the tools and we will finish the job."

Pointedly entitled HR 1776, Lend-Lease passed the Senate March 8, 1941, by 60-31. Like a timid bather, the United States was gradually getting its feet wet.

"BARBAROSSA"

1941

Directive 21 was so secret only nine copies were issued. But anyone familiar with "Mein Kampf" might have guessed its contents. It was Hitler's order to prepare to invade the Soviet Union.

Directive 21 and all that accompanied it was to enlarge World War II to a Satanic barbarity on a scale the world may never have witnessed. It engulfed perhaps 25 million lives. It was a final madness, and

Above: Horses were called into service with German supply trains as they vainly tried to keep the army equipped as it plunged ever deeper into the depths of the Soviet Union.

Left: The quick-step invasion of Russia eventually stalled as Germany ran out of fuel, food, clothing, ammunition—and out of time.

there are those who say only a madman could have issued it.

Adm. Wilhelm Canaris, head of the Abwehr, whose hatred of Hitler was well known and whose contacts with the Allies have never been fully explored, was appalled.

"The German army will bleed to death on the icy plains of Russia," he predicted. So had Napoleon in 1812. Guderian, the professional, saw Germany's perennial nightmare coming to pass once again. "So long as war in the West was undecided, any new undertaking must result in war on two fronts, and Adolf Hitler's Germany was even less capable of fighting such a war than had been the Germany of 1914." Gen. Friedrich Paulus, who was to live out his prediction at Stalingrad, said victory in Russia for Germany would be "beyond its capacity" unless the Red Army was annihilated and Moscow captured at once. In Paris, where he was commander of the German army in France, Gen. Johannes von

Blaskowitz spun a world globe, stopped it and pointed to the dot of Germany. "And all the rest? Tell me about hubris."

Even Nazi propaganda chief Josef Goebbels was privately uncertain. "Germany has never had luck in a two-front war. It won't be able to stand this one in the long run, either."

But Hitler had now styled himself the Grofaz —

Grosster Fedheer Allen Zeiten: greatest military commander of all time. He would bring to pass what he had written in "Mein Kampf": "If we talk about the new soil and territory in Europe today, we can think primarily only of Russia and its vassal border states ... The giant empire in the East is ready for collapse. And the end of the Jewish rule in Russia will also be the end of Russia as a state."

Stalin, every bit as much of a butcher as Hitler, had killed or intentionally starved as many as 10 million of his people in the '30s including 40,000 of his military in purges. Two weeks before Hitler invaded, Stalin executed the commander of his air force. But as inefficient as the communist machinery was, Russia produced 10 percent of the world's manufactures, was No. 2 in oil production, the leader in synthetic rubber.

After the flip-flop nonaggression pact in 1939, Stalin's stolid foreign minister, Vyacheslav Molotov, explained to the Supreme Soviet: "The political art in foreign affairs ... is to turn yesterday's enemies into good neighbors ... The Soviet Union and Germany were enemies. The situation is now changed, and we have stopped being enemies."

Hitler, the non-smoker, directed his propagandists to airbrush out Stalin's cigarettes in photos of the pact signing. But privately he said: "Everything I have in mind is directed against Russia. If the West is too stupid to understand this, then I will be forced to come to terms with Russia to crush the West and then ... turn with all my forces against the Soviet Union."

The Battle of Britain derailed the scenario but not the Fuhrer's will. Joachim von Ribbentrop, Hitler's foreign minister who was as bubble-headed as the champagne he used to sell, romanced Molotov in Berlin with fanciful promises of a warm water seaport. "Which sea?" asked Molotov stonily. Britain is defeated, Ribbentrop airily assured Molotov as they took shelter during an RAF air raid. "If that is so, why are we in this shelter and whose are those bombs which fall?" Molotov asked.

An anxious Stalin, buying time to rearm, offered to join the Axis. Hitler never even replied. His plans were too far along. He had begun planning for the attack in June 1940 even as his tanks still rolled through France. He assigned the details to Col. Bernhard von Lossberg whose outline ran 30 pages

At first, Operation Barbarossa was a walkover. Here Nazi troops enter Minsk. But winter came early in 1941, and the overextended blitzkrieg stalled.

The Yugoslav Josip Broz, known as Tito, was the war's most successful guerrilla leader. Tito, right, was a communist who fought not only the Nazis but royalist, anticommunist partisan leader Gen. Draza Mihailovich in a mini-civil war.

and was named "Fritz" for his son. Then the OKW refined it. Von Brauchitsch estimated the attack would take four weeks. Alfred Jodl, another of Hitler's "yes" generals, predicted: "The Russian colossus will prove to be a pig's bladder. Prick it and it will burst."

Directive 21 was signed by Hitler December 18, 1940. It was given a new name: Case Barbarossa. This was the nickname of Frederick I, a Holy Roman emperor who drowned in 1190 leading the Third Crusade and whose spirit was said to inhabit Kyfhauser Mountain in central Germany. Someday, according to folklore, he would emerge to lead Germany in the conquest of Europe.

Churchill, U.S. Undersecretary of State Sumner Welles, as well as his own master spy in Tokyo, Richard Sorge, all warned Stalin of an impending invasion. Genuine or not, Stalin dismissed all the reports as British-inspired rumors to divide the two dictators. Even a left-footed spy ring — and the Rote Kapelle (Red Orchestra) communist network in Germany was anything but — would have noted telltale signs. Germany was requisitioning farm horses. East Prussian farmers along the Soviet border had been ordered not to plant spring crops. By April 1941 there had been 80 invasions by German planes of Russian air space. A German photo plane made a forced landing 100 miles inside Russia. But Stalin loyally kept grain and oil trains running into Germany by the Moscow-Berlin express even early on

BALKANS

A factor in Hitler's failure to knock out Russia on schedule was an unanticipated delay in Yugoslavia. Bulgaria, Romania and Hungary had been muscled into the German camp and Yugoslavia, too, March 25, 1941. Two days later, an anti-Nazi coup installed King Peter. Enraged, Hitler let the Luftwaffe loose on Belgrade, killing 17,000 civilians. German troops swept through the country and Greece. A Commonwealth force of 60,000 Britons, Australians and New Zealanders landed in Greece April 5 but were beaten back to Athens where 50,000 survivors were evacuated April 29. But Mussolini's army had still not been able to cross the Greek frontier.

Some 28,000 Anzacs under Gen. Bernard Freyberg, an exotic New Zealander who had been a dentist in San Francisco and fought *with* Pancho Villa, took a stand in Crete. German paratroops, including boxer Max Schmeling, landed. Native peasants castrated some and beheaded others, but Germans kept coming, and May 30-31 the remaining 16,500 Allied soldiers were taken off in yet another evacuation.

Earlier, off Greece's Cape Matapan, the Royal Navy sank three Italian cruisers including the Pola, whose crew was so drunk they never fired a shot.

The fighting delayed Barbarossa a month, and furious partisan warfare broke out in Yugoslavia against German occupiers and between Tito's communist guerrillas, monarchists led by Draza Mihailovich and pro-Nazi Croats.

June 22, the day Sorge had radioed that Nazi Germany would strike.

Four days earlier, a German enlisted man, Alfred Liskof, who had been in a drunken fight with an officer, deserted and gave Russian front line troops the same date. Triggered by the codeword Dortmund, the German army roared into Russia at 3:30 a.m. June 22. Germany came with 148 divisions, 3 million men, 3,350 tanks, 7,100 cannon and 2,000 planes. Within days, 1,000 Soviet planes were destroyed — on the ground. By the second week in July, Guderian had captured 500,000 prisoners.

Smolensk fell August 5 with another 310,000 Russians, Kiev September 16 with 500,000 more.

Stalin said nothing for days other than to wail: "All that Lenin created we have lost forever." Churchill, on the other hand, called Hitler a "bloodthirsty guttersnipe" and said of the Stalin he despised: "If Hitler invaded hell, I would make at least a favorable reference to the Devil in the House of Commons." (Pope Pius XII said Germany was "defending the foundations of Christianity.")

Hitler had gambled yet again on blitzkrieg, but this time his strategy was flawed. Instead of sending the panzers ahead at full throttle, they were delayed to help the follow-up infantry deal with the huge masses of surrounded Russian soldiery. The Germans invaded with only a month's reserve of diesel fuel for the tanks. Hitler said all would soon be over. But rain made the few roads quagmires and the adjacent fields impassable. Each panzer division needed 300 tons of supplies a day. But 300 muddy miles from home and because of primitive railroads that had to be converted to the German gauge, some got only 70 tons. The Center Army Group of Gen. Fedor von Bock needed 25 trains a day but some days got only seven and on the best day 15. The Germans juggled four panzer groups when it needed six operating full time. Hitler did not have enough tanks for a war of encirclement, annihilation — and penetration. The blitz slowed.

"We misjudged the combat strength and combat efficiency of the enemy as well as our own troops," admitted Gen. H. von Greiffenberg, von Bock's chief of staff. "At the beginning we reckoned with some 200 enemy divisions," said Halder. "We have already identified 360. When a dozen of them are destroyed, the Russians throw in another dozen." (Germany made 3,790 tanks that year. Russia made 6,590.)

At first, Ukrainians and other ethnics who despised the Russians welcomed the invaders. But when they were massacred along with everyone else — more than a million Russian prisoners, perhaps 2 million, were shot or starved to death that first year — they became bitter partisans against the Germans. One act of vengeance as winter came was to tie captured Germans naked to trees, then douse them with water until they froze into human ice.

On October 2, von Bock launched 14 panzer divisions and three infantry armies in Operation

German infantrymen fought their way into Kiev in September 1940. Not far away SS murder squads were machine gunning 33,771 Jews to death in a ravine called Babi Yar.

Typhoon to take Moscow. The first snow fell October 4, unusually early. Then thaw. Then freeze. Temperatures hit minus-30 centigrade. Tankers had to light fires under their machines to get them started. Sorge correctly informed Moscow that the Japanese had decided to strike south instead of against Russia in Siberia, so 17 ski-equipped divisions were rushed westward. On November 27, however, Guderian was within 19 miles of Moscow, the city in sight. The government had fled to Kuibyshev, 688 miles east in the Urals. Hitler had told expectant Germans to register for Russian farmland. But in the alternate thaw and freeze, Red Army gun barrels glowed red hot as they fired incessantly. Guderian's soldiers, still in summer battledress at a time when the war was meant to be over, were crippled by frostbite and typhus. On December 5, Guderian, on his own,

LENINGRAD

On September 22, 1941, Leningrad was cut off and the longest siege of the war began. Food ran out, electricity failed and water came from holes chopped in the ice. Civilians were reduced to eating sheep gut jelly and pets and rodents and glue boiled off wallpaper. They burned books and furniture to stay warm. Rationing of whatever could come across the ice was draconian. People were shot for stealing a loaf of bread or ration cards. The starving fell dead in their tracks and lay frozen until spring. Families hid their dead to keep using their ration cards. Patties of human meat were sold illicitly. By January, 200,000 of the city's 2.5 million people had died, 1,300,000 by the time the 857-day siege was lifted January 27, 1944.

In 1941 a renewed Nazi offensive drove all the way to the Caucasus. Russian counterattacks as winter came soon had these troops in Rostov retreating as fast as they had come.

started falling back. The same day, Marshal Georgi Zhukov began a winter offensive that was to send the Germans reeling in reverse up to 100 miles.

The Moscow Circus opened its season on schedule that December. The jubilant ringmaster said Hitler would be unable to attend.

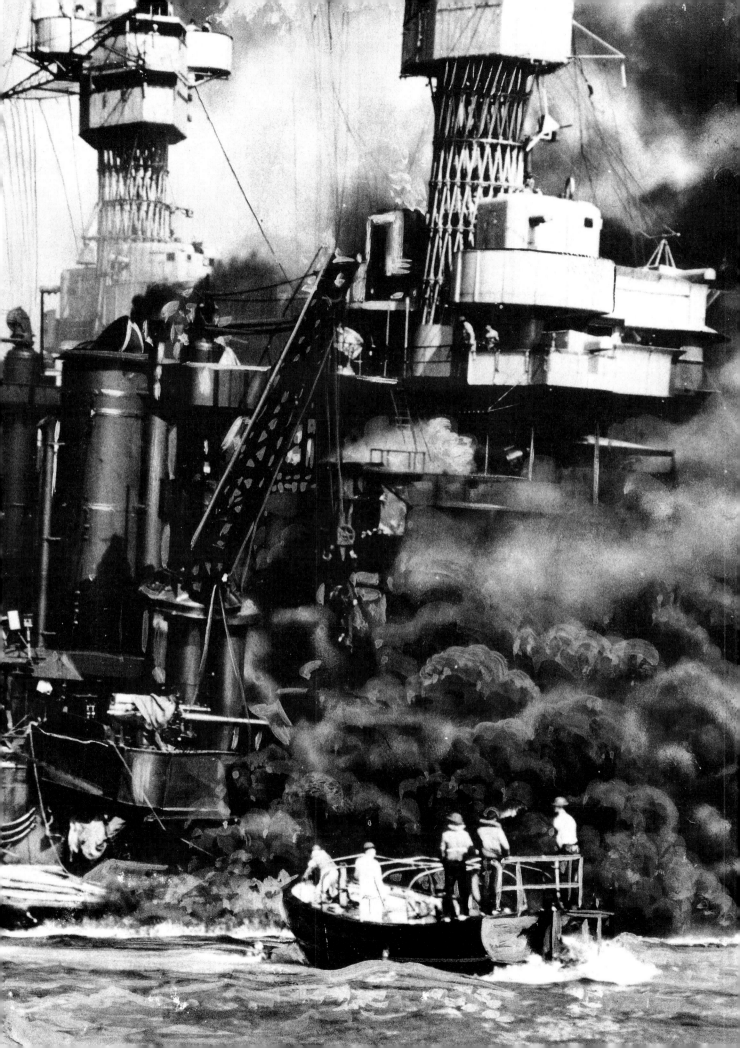

10

LINDY

1941

Odd it was that the first flier to solo across the Atlantic became the most outspoken believer that that ocean was wide enough to keep America out of Europe's war. Or should be wide enough.

Or maybe Charles Augustus Lindbergh was uniquely qualified to judge the security of isolation after his 33 1/2 hours to Paris. Howsoever, while the swastika's crooked tentacles enclosed Europe, Lindbergh became the figurehead of American non-involvement. The shy, introverted Lone Eagle was the son of a congressman but a political naif. Yet his speeches were of a piece with American traditions:

Above: *Charles A. Lindbergh lost his hero's wings as he passionately urged his countrymen to stay out of World War II.*

Left: *Ironically, the event that brought the U.S. into the war in Europe was the bombing of Pearl Harbor.*

Washington's warning against "entangling alliances," James Monroe's doctrine of hemispheric American hegemony. Read today, however, Lindbergh's speeches sound almost treasonous, certainly racist and, once, anti-Semitic.

Roosevelt had to contend with such pacifist voices as he took the oath of office for a third term January 20, 1941, his 300-year-old family Bible opened to First Corinthians, Chapter 13: "For now we see through a glass darkly..." George Marshall, who led the inaugural parade on horseback (he rode every morning if possible for quiet time), put his finger on Roosevelt's quandary: "A democracy has a very hard time in war, particularly at the start. They can never get ready in advance ... An arbitrary government like Hitler's (is) just bound to win at the start unless they [sic] are very, very stupid." Lindbergh made uniting the nation no easier.

After France fell, he declared: "The white nations of Europe should not destroy the western wall of

63

Detroit Tiger slugger Hank Greenberg traded in his $55,000 salary for a private's pay of $21 a month when he was drafted in 1941.

arms (i.e. Germany) which can hold back ... the infiltration of inferior blood." And: "The alternative to a negotiated peace is a Hitler victory or a prostrate Europe and possibly a prostrate America as well." And: Hitler "is undoubtedly a great man (but) fanatic in many ways...When conditions become as chaotic as they were in Germany after the war, one must expect fanaticism to result and hope that moderation comes later." And: "Since Germany was allowed to rearm, we should be prepared to accept the consequences of that rearmament including the readjustment of her eastern borders." All this from a man who had said a few years before: "Germany has no intention of attacking France for many years to come if at all."

Roosevelt's barbed-tongued Interior Secretary, Harold Ickes, called Lindbergh "the No. 1 Nazi fellow traveler...proud possessor of a Nazi decoration which has already been well earned (and who) would abjectly surrender his sword even before it is demanded." Roosevelt said one Lindbergh speech couldn't have done more for Nazism "if it had been written by Goebbels himself."

But Americans heeded Lindbergh, and not just America Firsters. He packed auditoriums across the country. But in Des Moines on September 11 he set off an uproar when he said: "If...the British, the Jewish or the administration stop agitating for war...there would be little danger of our involvement. Instead of agitating for war, the Jewish groups

MEANWHILE ... '41

A critic said a scrawny young band vocalist named Frank Sinatra sounded like a person having his toenails pulled out without anesthetic. Chevrolet introduced windshield spray on its 1941 models. FM began broadcasting. The FCC ordered CBS to program 15 hours a week of a new whatzit called television. Tennessee Williams eked out a living as a waiter and elevator operator in New York's Greenwich Village.

"Citizen Kane" got only one Oscar. Moviegoers preferred Judy Garland and Mickey Rooney in "Life Begins for Andy Hardy" or Ronald Reagan in "King's Row." George Raft turned down the role taken by Humphrey Bogart in "The Maltese Falcon" because "it wasn't a major picture."

The Animal Trap Co. of America got a $71,000 defense contract to make folding cots. Homing pigeon fanciers were asked to register their birds in case the phone lines were blitzed. Pitcher Hugh Mulcahy of the Phillies was the first big leaguer to be drafted. Right behind was Tiger slugger Hank Greenberg, trading in his $55,000 salary for a private's $21 a month. Back on the diamond, Joe DiMaggio hit in 56 straight games, Ted Williams batted .406 and Mickey Owen dropped a third strike.

Broadway packed them in for "Arsenic and Old Lace" and "Lady in the Dark." On Fifth Avenue, Anne Morrow Lindbergh was appalled at all the patriotic glitz in show windows, commenting that all it amounted to was "'Be brave' in diamonds."

in this country should be opposing it in every way for they would be among the first to feel its consequences."

One telegram to Lindbergh in reaction said: "Have just been reading a book called the Holy Bible. Has large circulation in this country. Written entirely by foreigners, mostly Jews."

In Washington, Roosevelt was confronted with the same possiblility that Hitler had just initiated: a two-front war. In July, Japan occupied French Indochina and was threatening the Dutch in oil-rich Sumatra. Roosevelt retaliated by freezing Japanese assets in the United States, in effect embargoing oil exports to that recent Axis partner. An attack by Japan on the United States, Britain or the Dutch somewhere in Asia was no longer a paper theory, no matter what Col. Lindbergh was saying.

Hitler, as it turned out, had already signed his death warrant with Directive 21. He showed equally blithe ignorance in a letter to Mussolini June 21, the day before Barbarossa began. "Whether or not America enters the war is a matter of indifference, as she is already helping our enemy with all the power she can muster." This was far from the mark. War production in the United States for the year was only $3 billion (multiply by eight to approximate 1993 dollars) of $47 billion authorized. Strikes at North American Aviation at Inglewood, California, held up $200 million in defense work, one at Federal Shipbuilding & Drydock in Kearny, New Jersey, $500 million. Roosevelt even threatened to draft the Jersey strikers.

By September, there were 1,443,500 men in the Army, but 987,000 of the draftees were soon eligible to leave. (And it was worrying that 45 percent of draftees had been rejected — 80 percent of Mississippians — the major causes being bad teeth, TB, and VD.) Roosevelt asked Congress to extend the draft. August 12, by a single vote, the House by 203-202 did so. One-year draftees stopped scrawling the graffito "OHIO" — Over the Hill in October — in barracks washrooms.

Roosevelt was not in town for the House vote. He was believed to be at sea fishing when actually he had rendezvoused with Churchill in Argentia Bay in Newfoundland. The cigar and the cigarette holder had been corresponding as two former naval officials since Churchill became Prime Minister. Churchill worried if the President would like him. He had sailed over on the battleship Prince of Wales. En route he watched the film "Lady Hamilton" for the fifth time and still cried over the tearjerker about Horatio Nelson's mistress. The two got along famously and issued the ringing but toothless Four Freedoms of the Atlantic Charter. But the tough talk concerned future military collaboration. Churchill's advisers assured the Americans that bombers and a blockade would suffice to conquer Germany. Marshall, in a stance that was to be argued heatedly right up to the Normandy invasion, was adamant. Victory in Europe would have to be won by the Allied foot soldier.

At that stage, none of the American military leaders inspired their British counterparts with confidence. To them the United States was totally unprepared and naive in the bargain.

This was only partially accurate when 400,000 soldiers went on maneuvers in Louisiana that autumn. True, white flags were waved to denote a cannon shot. Trucks bore the signs "Tank," cardboard tubes were "Mortars" and broomsticks "Machine Guns." But Col. Eisenhower proved brilliant at staff work as did Maj. Gen. Patton with his "tanks." Paratroops participated as well, their 'chutes, fortuitously, being the real thing. Mark Clark read off those lucky to get a general's star after the exercise. He called the officers back to read a name he had omitted, brand new Brig. Gen. Eisenhower. "I'll get you for this, you S.O.B," said Ike, showing the grin that was to get him more than stars.

All summer long, Maj. Albert C. Wedemeyer, a name to remember in Marshall's little black book, had been working on the Victory Program, an outline of what it would take to win the war. The result was remarkably prescient. Wedemeyer estimated an army of 8,795,658. The actual force in May 1945 was 8,291,336. The program estimated the United States was capable of extended offensive actions by July 1, 1943. Guadalcanal, in August, and North Africa, in November, were both invaded in 1942. And to FDR's question, yes, Hitler could be beaten.

Production on the home front wasn't that predictable. William Knudsen, ex-president of General Motors now federal production boss, was refused a sample of steel by the Quartermaster Corps because, having been born in Denmark, he was "a foreigner." Donald Nelson had mastered retailing at Sears Roebuck but encountered a mare's nest in allocating priorities to the nation. "In 1941 we almost lost the war before we even got into it."

Out in the Atlantic the United States skirted ever closer to outright shooting. "I am not willing to fire the first shot," Roosevelt declared, and Hitler for all his low regard for American potential, told his U-boats they shouldn't, either. But in February the President extended the American patrol area from home waters to 26 degrees West longitude, even with Iceland. In July, troops under Maj. Gen. Cortlandt Parker landed at Reykjavik, Iceland — "Rinkydink" to the men. British merchant ships were being repaired in U.S. yards and RAF pilots trained at American fields.

A Gallup poll said 41 percent of Americans favored U.S. convoying ships to Britain, 50 percent against. But if the alternative were the defeat of Britain, 71 percent were for it. In any event, the United States gave 2.5 million tons of merchantmen to the United Kingdom.

In September, Marshall was interrupted three times by phone calls while sawing a limb off an apple tree in his garden. He never finished it until the next spring. For war was literally just over the horizon. By the end of October, U.S. warships had escorted 14 convoys totalling 675 ships beyond Iceland. On October 17, the American destroyer Kearny was damaged by a torpedo. Eleven sailors died. On November 1, the old World War I rustbucket Reuben James, named for the sailor who saved Stephen Decatur's life at Tripoli in 1804, was torpedoed by a U-boat and sank with loss of 115 lives. Out in the Pacific, Douglas MacArthur had been alerted to the possibility of a Japanese attack. He was confident in the power of 35 Flying Fortresses, half of the total U.S. overseas force. And then came December 7.

Movie director John Ford was working with photo intelligence and dining at the old Alexandria, Virginia, home of Adm. Williams Pickens, the Navy's chief of navigation. The phone interrupted dinner that Sunday. Mrs. Pickens answered, listened, then lay the phone down. "It's no use getting excited," she said. "This is the seventh war that's been announced in this dining room."

Gen. Ira Eaker was roused from a nap by Mrs. Eaker. "The Japs bombed Pearl Harbor," she said. "You'll have to think up a better story to get me out of bed," the general yawned. She turned up the radio.

Pitcher Bob Feller was en route to the winter baseball meetings in Chicago. He called up Gene Tunney, head of the Navy's fitness program, offering to enlist immediately. At the meeting, general manager Bill DeWitt of the St. Louis Browns was downcast. He had hoped to move his usually hapless team to Los Angeles, now probably a war zone.

At his Wolf's Lair in a gloomy East Prussian forest, Hitler welcomed the surprising news. "We can't lose the war," he cried. "Now we have a partner who hasn't been defeated in 3,000 years." (He made certain he couldn't ever say as much by another fatal error. Although the United States had not declared war on Germany, he did on it, gratuitously, within four days.)

In London, de Gaulle, still with little more than his clothes and family photograph, said with foresight: "The war is over. Of course, there are years of fighting ahead, but the Germans are beaten."

A week after Pearl Harbor, America First announced it was disbanding. Had its principles been followed, it said in a parting shot, "war could have been avoided."

Lindbergh asked to be called to active duty in the Army Air Corps. Roosevelt turned him down.

11

Befehl ist Befehl

1941-42

I n German: *befehl ist befehl*. A translator put it in English for the Nuremburg tribunal: orders are orders. Orders: don't waste ammunition. Orders: place the bayonet at the neck vertebrae, sight down the barrel, fire. This was the most efficient method.

How did those who gave the orders know this? Worse: how did they know there would always be men who would follow these orders? Always. All day. All tomorrow. In Poland, in Russia, in 1941 and 1942. Always.

In "Julius Caesar," Shakespeare writes: "Cry 'Havoc!' and let slip the dogs of war." Havoc is a medieval word, an order to begin rapine and pillage. "Cry Havoc!" is not enough to describe Poland and Russia in 1941 and 1942. Lay the Jew down.

Left, above: Hitler's "Mein Kampf" come true. A small boy in Poland ... Jews in Warsaw. Both photos on these pages were evidence at the Nuremberg war crimes trial.

Point the bayonet just so. Shoot. Another neck. Another shot. Blood, gristle, brains explode all over the rifle, the shooter. Cigarette break. Back to work. All day. All tomorrow.

"Havoc!" explains nothing. Humans pulled the triggers on other humans. Not even wild beasts do this, massacre their own kind. Adolf Eichmann underwhelmed Hannah Arendt as "the banality of evil." Christropher Browning titles his book on a police unit that murdered 38,000 Jews with their guns "Ordinary Men." But what happened all day, all tomorrow was not banal, not ordinary. It is beyond definition. Perhaps it is best to follow the dying entreaty of 81-year-old Simon Dubnar, a famous historian and one of 25,000 Jews killed in Riga December 7-9, 1941. "Schreibt und farschreibt," he implored in Yiddish. Write and record.

Orders. The Germans are renowned for writing everything down. The orders for the Holocaust are a language of euphemism. Hitler's "under-

OTHERS

Germans were not alone in the slaughter. Some Balts and Ukrainians were willing collaborators. Hilfswillige, or Hiwis, "volunteers" recruited from Ukrainian, Latvian and Lithuanian POWs who were anti-Semites, joined the killing units. Hiwis used bullwhips to lash Jews into cattle cars en route to Treblinka. They also served as guards at the camps, camps where sometimes infants were hurled live into the ovens.

The camps were all remote but had convenient rail connections. Of Jews sent to Treblinka and Sobibor, none survived. Two did from Belzec, three from Chelmno. (One of them was among hundreds killed by anti-Semitic Poles after the war.) There were no survivors among 900 Jews at Novi Sad in Yugoslavia, either. They were driven onto the frozen Danube in January 1942, then the ice was shelled.

Women inmates at Auschwitz, photographed by a guard. The day Hitler shot himself, 1,000 prisoners who had been marched out of Theresienstadt in flight from the Russians were murdered by their German guards. The war ended a week later.

standing" with the Jews was something they well enough understood without having to read "Mein Kampf." They had understood ghettoes and pogroms for centuries. In World War II, German bureaucratese for transportation and extermination in the killing camps of Poland was "resettlement to the East." Massacres were "actions." The S.S. Einsatzgruppen who did the killing by trigger finger before the camps industrialized the process roughly translates as "groups on special mission."

Orders. Otto Ohlendorf, a smart, articulate, handsome young man, had been a rising star in the SS. He was put in charge of Einsatzgruppen D, one of four such killing teams. He testified at the Nuremberg war crimes trial that his men had killed 90,000 men, women and children in the year after Barbarossa began. Did he have any scruples about it? he was asked.

"Yes, of course (but) ... it is inconceivable that a subordinate should not carry out orders given by leaders of the state."

The Nazis had demonstrated they were bloody-minded enough with their own people. As soon as the war broke out, Hitler ordered the elderly and insane in hospitals to be "taken care of" to make room for war wounded. As many as 100,000 were killed before word leaked out, the clergy protested and "Aktion 4" was stopped.

Early in 1940, 300 Jews under the direction of a man named Rudolf Hoess began cleaning up an old Austro-Hungarian barracks in the Polish town of Oswiecim. The Germans called it Auschwitz. It was to be a site for an I.G. Farben synthetic rubber plant worked by slave labor. The first workers who moved into new barracks next to the factory were 708 Poles from the Tarnow jail. There was room for many more. Elsewhere in occupied Poland, rumors of atrocities circulated almost as soon as the Germans moved in. A cardinal reported to the Pope February 11, 1940, that "with few exceptions (the

Rubble of the Warsaw ghetto. It and its inhabitants were mercilessly wiped out by the SS afn an uprising against the German occupation.

Germans) are only executioners and sadists." The ambivelance of the Vatican during the Holocaust is still debated.

Just before Barbarossa was launched, Goering instructed Reinhard Heydrich, son of a music teacher and, as head of the Reich Security Office, the right hand man to SS chief Heinrich Himmler, to plan "the final solution to the Jewish question." About 20,000 men were recruited from the SS and Gestapo to form the Einsatzgruppen and began machine pistol training in Saxony. "No more than two bullets per Jew," Himmler ordered. With Teutonic thoroughness, and foresight, the soldiers were removed from the jurisdiction of military courts.

The "special units" followed hard on the heels of the invading German army into the lands of the old Russian Pale where Jews had been relocated by the czars over a century before. Hardly had Bialystok, half Jewish, been captured, than the city's Jewish elders pleaded for their people. German officers

urinated on the kneeling supplicants and torched 700 Jews in a synagogue. On July 12, the remaining Jews were marched to anti-tank ditches outside town. The executions went on all day and into the evening under truck headlights. The officers provided "social events" that night to blot out "the impressions of the day." Killing resumed next day and the ditches filled in, graves now "not to be known."

A Jew in Kedainiai bit an SS soldier in the throat August 28, killing him. Two thousand Jews were shot in retaliation. In Ejszyszki 3,400 Jews were executed September 27, 10,000 in Vinnitsa five days earlier. When the Germans captured Kiev, all of the city's Jews were corralled and herded to Babi Yar, a ravine in the woods beyond the city. Stripped, they were taken to the edge of a pit and machine gunned until the huge excavation became a moaning, writhing mass of the dead and dying. A few feigned death and escaped in the dark, but 33,771 died in Babi Yar that September 27-28. By the end of August, one of the four Einsatzgruppen methodically reported it had killed 229,051 Jews.

The killing was not confined to Russia. In Hungary, Iron Guard fascists slashed the throats of Jews and burned others alive. Vichy France built eight concentration camps and barred Jews from high office.

Heydrich called a meeting at Wannsee outside Berlin January 20, 1942, to make the killing more systematic. The final solution, he said, would involve not only Jews under German jurisdiction but all the Jews of Europe including Britain and down to the 3,000 in Portugal. "A total of 11 million will have to fall away."

Eichmann was put in charge of transporting Jews for "resettlement." He had witnessed one mass execution and could not stomach another. "There are men who can look upon such actions. I cannot. At night I cannot sleep. I dream. I cannot do it." He was to testify he had never seen a written order. "All I know is that Heydrich told me, 'The Fuhrer has ordered the physical extermination of the Jews.'" Befehl ist befehl.

On the day the Japanese bombed Pearl Harbor, the Germans experimented outside Chelmno by killing Jews locked in trucks with exhaust fumes. It worked but was wasteful of gasoline.

Firing squads, also, were too inefficient. And too public. In March 1942, Heydrich ordered construction of a death camp at Bergen-Belsen, in April at Sobibor, in June at Auschwitz. Meanwhile gunfire would be the instrument of necessity in a renewed Operation Heydrich. By March, 20 to 25 percent of the Jews who were to die had been killed. A year later, when the gas chambers came on line, the percentage was reversed.

Lodz' ghetto contained 200,000 Jews before the war, the second largest in Europe. Only 10,000 somehow survived. So, hidden away, did the chronicles of their dying. Day by day they starved, were shot behind the barbed wire. "Listen and believe this even though it happened to the wife of Dr. Tzamber ..." wrote Jozef Zelkowicz.

A German officer insisted on taking her child, a wasteful mouth to feed, from Mrs. Tzamber.

"The suckling must be taken away."

"No!"

"Really? Truly?" The officer told the mother to turn away and shot both in the head.

By June 18, 100,000 Jews had been murdered in Lublin, 65,000 in Cracow. There had been a shortage of railroad cars, so Jews were killed without resettlement.

The "ordinary men" of Browning's book were Reserve Police Battalion 101, part-time officers who had been leading mundane lives back in Hamburg. They went into action at Josefow near Lublin in July 1942. Some men were allowed to withdraw from the execution squads. Others tried to look busy elsewhere. But there were always enough. Said one: "The shooters were grievously besmirched with blood and brains and bone splinters." They relaxed for lunch, then resumed work. That night no one discussed the day's events, killing one by one 1,500 Jews. Everyone got drunk. "My neighbor shot the mother, and I shot the child ... I reasoned, after all, without its mother the child could not live any longer." One officer with the 101st brought his new wife out on their honeymoon.

The words of a guard on a train to Lvov in the fall of 1942 when Hitler was gambling all and needed all on a drive to Stalingrad: "On September 8, some 300 Jews — old and weak, ill, frail and no longer transportable — were executed... Only in exceptional cases were pistols used." Jews kept breaking out of the stinking cars. Stationmasters farther down the line were telegraphed ahead for boards and nails. Eventually the guards ran out of ammunition. "So for the rest of the journey (we) had to resort to stones ... and bayonets."

Schreibt und farschreibt.

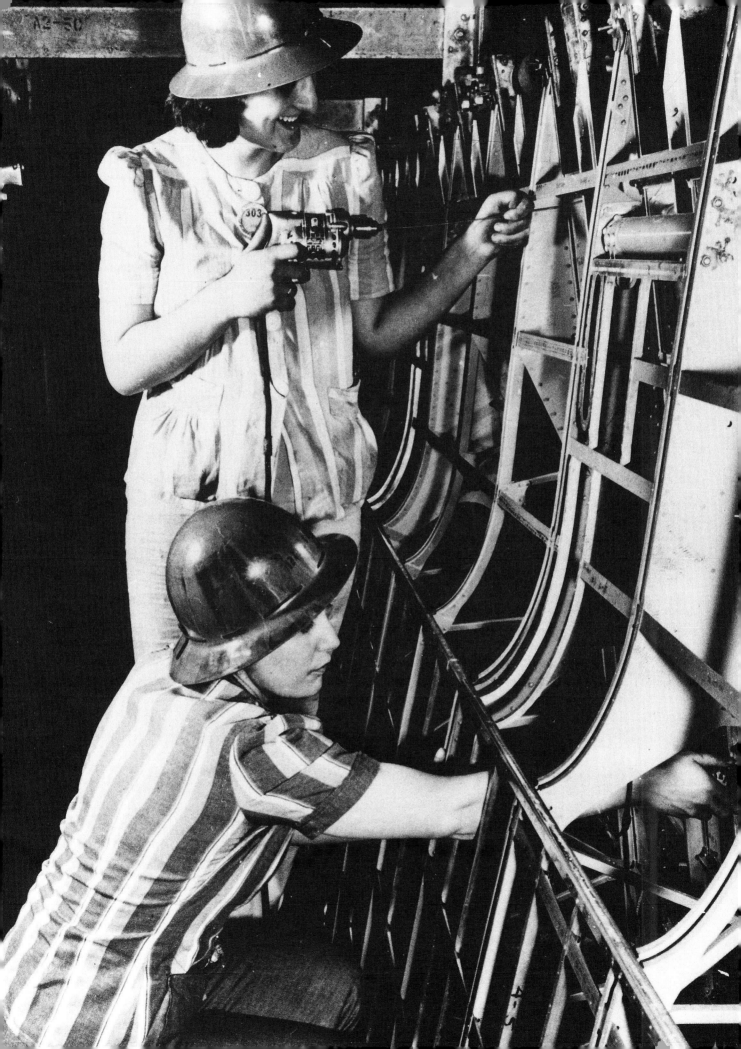

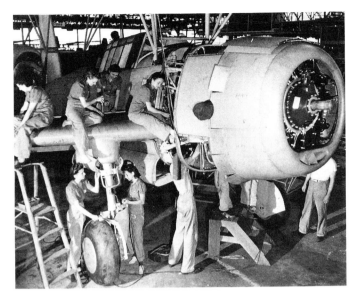

12

"TORCH"

1942

In the first six months of a war with Great Britain and the United States, I will run wild and win victory after victory," predicted Adm. Isoroku Yamamoto, architect of the Pearl Harbor attack. "But then, if war continues two or three years after that, I have no confidence in our ultimate victory."

Yamamoto was a prophet but also a gambler, a real one. He had loved to play poker and bridge for high stakes as a student at Harvard and later as a naval attache in the Japanese embassy in Washington.

A better prophet and one not heeded was Rear

Above: *Men flew them, but women built them. Female workers fabricate a dive bomber on a Nashville assembly line.*

Left: *Rosie the Riveter became a symbol of overwhelming American production and the acceptance of women on the assembly line.*

Adm. Takijiro Onishi, chief of staff of the 11th Japanese Air Fleet. Attacking the Philippines was one thing, he warned, but hitting Pearl Harbor would make the Americans "insanely mad." Just so.

America became a nation of Minutemen all over again. Recruiting offices were swamped. Yamamoto's forecast was indeed fulfilled as the Japanese swept over Wake Island, Hong Kong, Bataan and Corregidor in the Philippines, Dutch East Indies, Malaya and Singapore, Burma. But the United States quickly girded for a long haul.

To save rubber now that East Asia was overrun, the government instituted gas rationing and imposed a 34 mph speed limit. The basic "A" ration gave motorists four gallons a week, later three. Harold Ickes picked up a door mat on the way out of the White House and donated it to a scrap rubber drive. Chiropodists howled because they didn't get the bountiful "C" card like medical doctors. Churchgoing didn't qualify for more gas, either. Average

Volunteer spotters man the top of the Empire State Building watching for enemy planes that never came.

highway mileage dropped from 19,663 per motorist in 1941 to 6,366 two years later. Stanley Steamers reappeared on the road. Sugar, then meat, coffee and other basics were rationed. Members of Detroit's murderous Purple Gang were arrested in Boston with a load of counterfeit ration stamps sewed into their clothing. Chester Bowles, director of the Office of Price Administration, sized up the performance of his fellow Americans and decided 3 to 5 percent were "inherently dishonest," 20 percent obeyed the laws and 75 percent "would like to."

Now that America was officially in the war, Churchill arrived in Washington via the battleship Duke of York December 22, 1941, to begin the Arcadia conference between the two high commands. The

Prime Minister was a guest at the White House. Roosevelt wanted to talk to Churchill after dinner one night when the Briton liked to take to a hot tub and a brandy and mammoth cigar. Roosevelt wheeled himself down the hall and knocked, then apologized if he was intruding. "Come in, Mr. President," called the P.M. "Great Britain has nothing to hide."

Actually, the Americans weren't so sure. Both Britain and the United States were now in the war together. But the Americans long held — largely to themselves — suspicions that "perfidious Albion" had ulterior motives beyond defeating the Axis: preserving its empire, hegemony in Europe. Necessarily diplomatic towards the potential might of their redeemer, the British were nonetheless appalled at the military reality of their new ally. The Americans lacked "even the slightest conception of what war means, and their armed forces are more unready than it is possible to imagine," said Sir John Dill, recently head of the Imperial General Staff who accompanied Churchill to Arcadia.

When Dill's successor, Sir Alan Brooke, met Marshall, he thought him affable enough, "but I shouldn't put him down as a great man." Marshall in turn didn't think Brooke matched Dill's intellect. Both men were to revise their opinions upwards in time.

The most important decision of Arcadia — and one of the biggest of the war — was to confirm Dog. Germany was the foremost enemy, and the European conflict would receive priority over the Pacific. This was a particularly hard choice for the Americans to swallow. The Japanese, not Adolf Hitler, had bombed Pearl Harbor, and that was what had made the Americans fighting mad. Subordinating the Pacific to Europe was a divisive issue that was long to haunt coordination of the allied commands.

Fortunately, one of the wisest decisions at Arcadia was to name the personable Dill as permanent British representative on the new Joint Chiefs of Staff to be based in Washington. Dill was a continuing voice of reason and partnership on both sides of the Atlantic and became very close, personally as well as militarily, to Marshall. Indeed, when later in the war Marshall picked up rumors that Churchill wanted to replace Dill, his American friend promptly arranged for him to be applauded with honorary degrees from Yale, William and Mary and elsewhere.

"Dill must be doing quite a job over there," said the unsuspecting Prime Minister. True, and when he died November 2, 1944, he became the first non-American to be buried in Arlington Cemetery.

Arcadia was a first glimpse at an inevitable conflict of interest between London and Washington. Marshall steadfastly — and in Britain's view, stubbornly — maintained France should be invaded as soon as feasible. This would ease the pressure on Russia and free U.S. forces all the sooner to concentrate against Japan where the nation's emotions were focused. Britain, its empire gone or beset, had limited men and money. It poised like a reluctant swimmer on the edge of the Channel, fearful of plunging into France and losing the one army it could afford. The Americans, who were to have 5,397,000 men in the army by the end of 1942 with more coming, were unsympathetic to British constraint. But Britain was the senior partner. Only gradually, as American arms became predominant, did the roles reverse.

Then there was Winston. He had, wrote an English historian, "a gusto for war." As a child, he played with his 1,500 toy soldiers. As a youth, he fought in Britain's last cavalry charge, at the Battle of Omdurman in the Sudan in 1898. He made a daredevil escape during the Boer War. He fancied himself, sometimes with reason, a military strategist without peer. But he could also dash off on crackpot flights of fancy that were the despair of his generals. They connived at any length to keep him from collaring Roosevelt in private and convincing him of some new knight errancy, FDR being something of a wheelchair warrior himself.

Adm. Ernest King, head of the U.S. Navy, favored the Pacific and didn't care who knew it. "My father is the most even-tempered man I know," said one of his daughters. "He's always in a rage." Roosevelt, too, was cool about France but wanted some action somewhere in 1942. There was a congressional election in November for starters, and he had to show something to the voters.

Eisenhower, head of the plans division in the War Department, had proposed "Sledgehammer," establishing a foothold in Brittany in 1942 with mostly British troops and enough of them to draw some Germans away from Russia. After a buildup in Britain of American forces —"Bolero"— a full-scale invasion of France —"Roundup"— would kick off in 1943. Marshall flew to England in the spring of 1942 to plead for Roundup after getting "the cigarette holder gesture" from Roosevelt when he counselled against too many operations in too many places around the globe. The Brits turned down Sledgehammer flat. As a sop, they came on board for Roundup but really did so just to buy time. As a compromise, they offered "Torch," an invasion of French North Africa. Marshall thought Churchill had been hunting soft underbellies again and wanted the United States to pull Britain's chestnuts out of the fire by chasing the enemy away from the Mediterranean and Suez. He gave Torch a 50-50 chance of success. Defeat in Africa would be unac-

Two of Germany's best, Field Marshal Erwin Rommel, in jodhpurs, a master of offense, and Field Marshal Albert Kesselring, left, a master of defense. Here they have the British on the run in Libya.

ceptable to the American people, he reasoned. Repulse of Sledgehammer would at least show the Allies were trying.

But he was overruled by higher powers. On July 25, 1942, plans for Torch got under way. A surprised Eisenhower was told to stop his paperwork. Instead, he would command the invasion.

* * * *

Before Torch, the battle in Africa was a yo-yo war. The endless deserts between Alexandria in Egypt and Tripoli in Libya were made-in-heaven tank country but for the sand that infiltrated everthing from trucks to teeth. Fuel had to be carried over hundreds of miles of sometimes roadless tracts. Men had to subsist on a gallon of water a day: for shaving, for washing a different fraction of the body in daily rotation, for brewing tea. The residue was

filtered and poured into tank radiators. British oil in Iraq and Iran plus the Suez Canal were the prizes. In June 1939, one of Britain's least heralded but best wartime generals, Sir Archibald Wavell, arrived in Cairo to organize a Middle East Command. The opponent was Italian, which sometimes fought bravely, sometimes not. On September 13, 1940, Marshal Rodolfo Graziani began the round-robin by striking into Egypt. He stopped 60 miles inside the border at Sidi Barrani to erect a monument to his glorious victory, then paused. Mistake. The next move was Lt. Gen. Sir Richard O'Connor's, who, with half as many Desert Rats, as the Commonwealth troops described themselves, struck the Italians from the rear. They proceeded to advance 500 miles to Benghazi.

"What time do the pubs close in this town?"

GONDAR

In a backwater campaign, a British Empire army of 21,500 men had been fighting against an Italian force of 350,000 to clear the Red Sea and Gulf of Aden. In a brilliant campaign of movement, they had marched 1,000 miles out of Kenya through Eritrea, Somaliland and into Ethiopia. The last of the Italians capitulated at Gondar in Ethiopia November 27, 1941.

For the New Zealanders in the army, it was sweet victory. The tiny nation had proportionately suffered the most casualties of any belligerent in World War I, and in World War II had the highest per capita number of men in its armed forces, second to the Soviet Union.

asked an Aussie. The Desert Rats took 135,000 prisoners who delighted their captors by cooking them pasta specialties.

The rout was too much for the Fuhrer. On February 20, 1941, Rommel landed in Libya with some of his panzers. Desert warfare was about to become a classic for future war colleges.

Rommel looked as much at home atop his tank as the Marlboro Man on his horse: his tunic and face caked with dust, his eyes piercing through the grime like a sheik's falcon, his goggles (eventually he was to wear the captured O'Connor's as, he said, "the booty of war") at the ready above the visor of his hat. Son and grandson of school teachers, he had chosen the military life. His World War I heroics make Rambo's seem pale. He was awarded the Pour le Merite, Germany's equivalent of the Medal of Honor for junior officers. His post as head of Hitler's bodyguard and blitzing through France won him promotion to a tanker's field of dreams. Britain's 8th Army had been reduced by two divisions, four air squadrons and 100 tanks sent to fight the Japanese when Rommel's Afrika Korps jumped off, retaking Benghazi April 4, 1941, and reaching the Egyptian border on the 28th. Bypassed was an Australian division holed up in Tobruk which withstood an illustrious 242-day siege. Feinting here, hitting there, Rommel pushed the British back into Egypt. Fighting was dust and confusion. Rommel even slept one night behind enemy lines near British headquarters. By December, a reinforced 8th Army

had gone the other way, relieving Tobruk and recapturing Benghazi only to be driven back in January by a renewed and elusive counterattack which seized Tobruk in June 1942 in only three days and finally was fought to a standstill by Sir Claude Auchinleck in heavy combat deep in Egypt at El Alamein. Churchill, grumpy over the heavy loss for his coalition government in a by-election, was only too happy to accept Auchinleck's resignation. Enter Sir Bernard Law Montgomery.

The British came to love their "Monty." The Americans did not return the favor. Son of a minister, he was an egocentric, arrogant and aesthetic soldier in the mold of Oliver Cromwell and Stonewall Jackson. He had a brave record in the first war, was badly wounded and later served in India where he stood out for eschewing both strong waters and polo. He stressed the training of men and tactics that would never again repeat the slaughterhouses of the World War I trenches. And he was a fighter. Rather than diplomatically play his scrubs as ordered in a soccer match against the crew of a German warship visiting India, he played the varsity, winning by almost room temperature. "I was taking no chances with those bastards," he explained.

When he first met Eisenhower, he turned to his blackboard to explain a point. His nose twitched. "Who's smoking?" he demanded. "I am, sir," said Ike. "Stop it. I don't permit it." Eisenhower never smoked in his presence again.

By October 1942, Montgomery had cautiously — a trademark — built up the 8th Army to a preponderance: 210,000 men, 1,100 tanks. Rommel, the Desert Fox, had once routed a much larger force with but 60 tanks and 2,500 men combined with brilliance. But he was outmanned, outgunned and undersupplied when Montgomery pounced October 17, 1942, after an unprecedented artillery barrage. Ralph Muller, an American with the American Field Service, was there.

"Jerry opened up with everything he had.... At a steady walk with their rifles at the port, (the infantry) marched into it looking straight ahead. I saw men with their heads blown off as they walked, men with arms and legs shot away.... There was no hope of getting through, but they kept on, wave after wave of them, and they marched in singing."

On November 4, the British broke through the minefields and iron defense of the German 88s, the

"JUBILEE"

Hitler guessed it, German intelligence confirmed it and troops were ordered to sleep in their battle gear. So when 6,000 soldiers, most of them Canadian, stormed ashore at the Channel port of Dieppe August 19, 1942, in a test of German defense and Allied offense, it was a slaughter. The troops hardly got off the beach. Casualties ran almost 60 percent before the remainder were withdrawn. Whether intended by the invasion-wary British as proof to the invasion-eager Americans of the peril of invading France, and some say it was, Sir Alan Brooke pointedly commented: "It is a lesson to the people who are clamoring for the invasion of France."

war's best cannon, and into open desert. Rommel and Montgomery would be wed forever in military history, but now the Desert Fox began a thousand-mile retreat. It was an ebbing, first of many, back from a high tide line, an ebbing back into the darkness of Germany from where the flow had come.

* * * *

As he boarded his transport in Norfolk, Maj. Gen. George Patton, commander of Operation Torch's Western Task Force, told the Navy he'd win if they could get him to within a week and 50 miles of his landing target at Casablanca. (The Navy arrived precisely and almost to the minute.) He was sailing with 24,500 men on 102 ships all the way across the Atlantic to invade Morocco. Other Americans from Britain were to land at Oran and an Anglo-American force at Algiers. All were under Eisenhower, the new theater commander. (The Americans would go in first. The French in North Africa still smoldered over Britain's attack on their fleet.)

Patton had some reason for unease. Aboard the

The Germans were waiting for the commando raid on Dieppe in 1942, stifling it on the beaches and taking this haul of, largely Canadian, prisoners. Some Americans thought the British did it to show the futility of invading France too soon.

escorting cruiser Brooklyn, only nine of 65 officers had more than three years of service, and half the crew had never been to sea. The escort carrier Suwannee was loaded with ammunition while it was still being completed in the shipyard. Torch was not only putting Marshall's new army to its maiden test. It was also landing in a thicket of intrigue: would the French in Morocco and Algiers fight for

German-tilting Vichy, de Gaulle, the Allies or none of the above?

To find out, Maj. Gen. Mark Clark had flown to Gibraltar in October (on the B-17 "Red Gremlin" piloted by one of the Air Corps' best, Paul Tibbets, who later flew the plane that dropped the atomic bomb on Hiroshima). From there, Clark took a submarine to Algeria to feel out French leaders. At one point, the conferees hid in a wine cellar when pro-Vichyites knocked on the door. Clark offered a Frenchman some chewing gum to keep him from coughing. It tasted stale, he said.

"Small wonder. I've been chewing it for two hours."

Patton's men hit the beaches at three points at Casablanca November 8, 1942, on one of the rare

days when the surf was down. Roosevelt was miffed it was too late for the election. One transport was torpedoed and its landing craft motored 100 miles to the beach. The French fleet sortied. Four of its destroyers were sunk. The new battleship Massachusetts, one of three with the American flotilla, silenced the French battleship Jean Bart within minutes and in like manner the Americans overcame French resistance.

German spies spotted the other invasion force from Tangiers as it entered the Mediterranean. They concluded it was en route to reinforcing Malta. The armada behaved as if this were so, then doubled back.

At Oran, 100 Americans were lost when French shore batteries sunk a converted Coast Guard cutter as it entered the harbor. Resistance was soon overcome and street urchins happily chanted the Ameri-

SAND

Consternation flustered the Allies when an officer carrying plans for Torch in an inside coat pocket was shot down off the coast of Spain. The Spanish recovered the body and turned it over to the British. The plans were still there. Sand in the buttonholes had not been disturbed, so the British decided the invasion had not been compromised by the pro-Axis Franco government.

can password-countersign "Heigh-ho, Silver — Away" as they lobbied for the GI's candy.

By coincidence, Adm. Jean-Francois Darlan, commander of all Vichy armed forces, happened to be in Algiers visiting his son who was stricken with

British and American forces contain an Axis drive in northeast Africa in the late summer of 1942. 1. A German drive through a British mine field near El Himeimat. 2. An Italian "assault" which was stopped soon after it started.

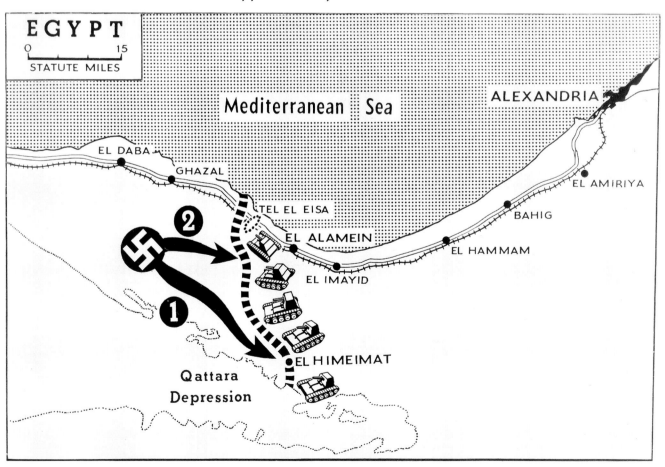

The Italians had little stomach for Hitler's and Mussolini's war and surrendered in crowds to Britain's Eighth Army.

polio. The Allies were warned that Darlan, whose great-grandfather had been killed by British cannon fire at Trafalgar, was not to be trusted, "not even with his daughter's chastity belt."

The Allies thereupon dithered in a "who's on first?" routine to win over the 100,000 Vichy soldiers in North Africa. Their commander, Gen. Alphonse Juin, said he would only obey orders from Marshal Petain in Vichy (which was occupied by the Nazis as soon as the Allies landed). De Gaulle had not been told of Torch at all, being deemed a red flag to the Vichyites, and was a towering inferno. Clark and U.S. diplomat Robert Murphy romanced Darlan, offering to take his son to Warm Springs, Georgia, and its polio spa created by fellow polio sufferer, FDR, as well as make the admiral high commissioner for Africa. The deal disgusted many. "I was not proud of (it)," Marshall said. But on November 10, Darlan defied Petain and ordered the North African French to turn their guns 180 degrees and

shoot Germans who were being hurriedly flown into Tunisia. (An assassin removed Darlan from the scene that Christmas Eve.)

Sir Kenneth Anderson drove his English troops 500 miles in a week, but when he reached the Tunisian border there were enough Axis forces to stop him. Rommel, who had been fighting a feinting retreat against the overly cautious pursuit of Montgomery, thought reinforcing Tunisia was "pure suicide." He was right, but on February 14, 1943, he decided to teach the pea-green U.S. troops a lesson. His tanks charged across the rocky scrub to Kasserine Pass in west central Tunisia. An American colonel reported he was "just shifting positions." "Shifting positions, hell! I know panic when I see it," snorted Col. Thomas Drake.

Capt. Allerton Cushman, an observer studying U.S. anti-tank weapons, watched the rout. "As far as I could see were clouds of dust as vehicles raced away from the advancing enemy. I opened my

The Allied triumph in Tunisia snared 250,000 prisoners, mostly Germans, because Hitler refused to evacuate them from a losing battle.

camera. After all, I was an observer. But I couldn't bring myself to press the shutter. It was too awful a sight."

Lt. Larry Marcus, of the Dallas merchant family, manned an experimental mobile weapon, a 37 mm peashooter mounted in a pickup truck. A Tiger tank with its 88 mm cannon routed Marcus's platoon. He escaped by crawling 16 miles, eating a letter from home en route. He figured the Germans would discover he was Jewish and kill him.

Maj. Gen. Lloyd Fredendall, a brusque, sloganeering know-it-all, commanded the American II Corps from a cave far behind the lines. Conditions in the command were suggested by one password, the unprintable GI acronym "Snafu" followed by "Damn right."

In two days, the 1st Armored Division lost 98 tanks. "The men didn't realize the brutality of war ... until things landed in their laps," Marshall reflected. "The American gives up as soon as he is attacked," the Germans observed. But a unit under British Brig. Charles Dunphy fought a dogged rearguard action as Brig. Gen. LeRoy Irwin sped 735 miles in four days with 48 cannon. Rommel withdrew —"lost his nerve," one critic has written — with the observation: "What really was amazing was the speed with which the Americans adapted themselves to modern warfare."

The lessons of Kasserine were immediate. Back in the United States, basic training was extended from 13 to 17 weeks. Fredendall was sacked and replaced by Patton. Neat dress including ties became the uniform of the day along with drill, drill, drill. But the general with the ivory-handled revolvers and shining helmet liner with gleaming silver stars also made certain his men got regular mail, hot meals and swing music on the radio.

Marshall knew Patton was an eccentric who could "curse, then write a hymn," said Marshall's biographer, Forrest Pogue. "But he saw behind his adolescent caperings the skill of a professional."

Overruling Anderson's doubts, Patton and his deputy, Omar Bradley, insisted the 35th Division participate in the final attacks on Tunis and Bizerte. The division stayed in the front lines for the next 605 days.

Confronted by Montgomery in the south of Tunisia, the Americans and French in the middle and more Britons in the north, Rommel pleaded for

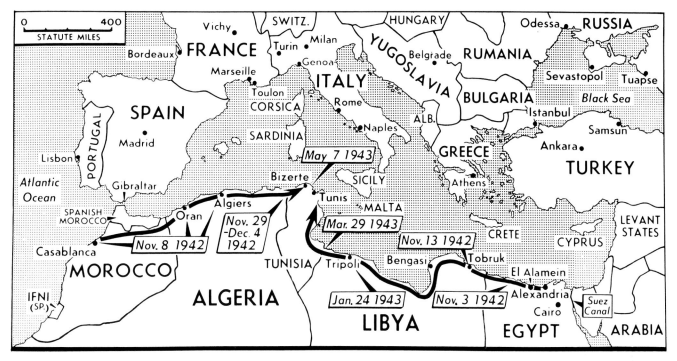

Allied drive through North Africa.

permission to shorten his lines. Hitler said no. After years of having his way, outbluffing his enemies, blitzkrieging them, retreat had become a fixation in the mind of this Grofaz, who considered himself the greatest military commander of all time. Not one step backwards. Not one. In March he ordered Rommel home. But he kept pouring men into Tunisia. Thus, when the Allies simultaneously captured Tunis and Bizerte May 7, 1943, they bagged 250,000 prisoners, a majority of them German. It had been folly. At the end the Allies were landing 400,000 tons

of war materiel a month in North Africa. The Germans got only 29,000 tons past Allied planes and warships. Tanks of the once proud Afrika Korps had only enough fuel for 25 kilometers. The results were all but preordained to any mind but a Grofaz's.

Hitler's prolonged defeat had given the Americans an unintended gift. It had provided invaluable training under game conditions. After Kasserine, said Eisenhower, his GIs were "mad and ready to fight." Torch had cost 70,000 Allied casualties, but now, finally, Germany was on the defensive.

Left: *Field Marshal Erwin Rommel in his usual pose, in a tank at the front. But, for a change, he has stopped temporarily.*

"WINTERGEWITTER"

1942-43

There is a Russian joke. A man tells his friend he has captured a bear. "Bring it so we can see it," says the friend. "I can't," is the reply. "The bear won't let me."

In the summer of 1942, Germany chased the bear almost into Asia. In the south, panzers drove 600 miles reaching the Caucasus within 100 miles of the Caspian Sea and the crucial oil fields of Baku. A propaganda team planted the swastika atop Mt. Elbrus, the highest peak in Europe. The smaller Maikop oil field had fallen but was left useless by

Above: General Winter was Russia's best ally as its peasant army pressed relentlessly against the freezing, underequipped Nazi army.

Left: Starving, beaten German prisoners surrender at Stalingrad. Of some 195,000 captives in all, only 6,000 lived to return home.

the departing Russians. Ironically, with oil under their feet the Germans were using camels to haul fuel for the tanks. Their advance had been astounding, but now the Germans were far from home fighting an enemy in the mountains who was defending his. Now Hitler sacrificed their mobility to concentrate on another fixation: Stalingrad.

"I want to get to the Volga," said the Fuhrer, "at a particular point where stands a certain town. By chance it bears the name of Stalin himself." The house professional, OKW Chief of Staff Halder, tried to keep Hitler out of "cloud cuckooland" by urging him to withdraw to less exposed, more defensible lines. In September, the Fuhrer fired him. Germans had reached the Volga August 23. On October 14, Hitler ordered the 250,000 men of Paulus's Sixth Army to march the remaining few miles to Stalingrad.

Once Tsaritsyn (and today Volgograd), the city of 600,000 had been renamed when Stalin organized

In Stalingrad, officers ponder their encirclement by Soviet armies. They are among the lucky few with winter clothing.

its defenses during the Russian civil war to cement the revolution. The Germans had come with Romanians, Italians, Hungarians and volunteers from France and Spain. But Paulus massed Germans for the strike, leaving his flanks to less reliable Romanians. Six hundred Luftwaffe bombers set the city aflame — and unintentionally made the city with no natural defenses a fortress from the resulting rubble. The 20,000 defenders of the 62nd Army took cover in basements and piles of debris and killed 3,000 Germans that first day at the Stalin Tractor Plant in one attack alone.

"We shall either hold the city or die there," declared Gen. V.I. Chuikov, the commander. "And before you die, kill a German, with your teeth if necessary." Bombs and shells from Russian artillery a mile across the river raised so much dust that visibility was just 100 yards.

"It was one continuous roar," said Chuikov. "In our dugout a tumbler would fly into a thousand pieces from vibration." Sixty-five men were killed in Chuikov's headquarters alone. One building changed hands five times in a day. A war of hundreds of kilometers became a war of meters. "There was fierce action for every wall or cellar and even for every heap of rubble," said Gen. Hans Dorr. The Russians tried to huddle within a grenade's throw of the Germans so they wouldn't be bombed. At night, boats ferried in reinforcements 20 or so at a time. Half might be killed before they could get into action. A regiment already reduced to 250 Russians had been cut down to six by November 11 when Germans held 90 percent of the city, reducing the Russians to a 1,000-yard toehold which they cut in two. But, in exhaustion, the offensive went on hold November 12.

Across the Volga, Russians nervously waited for the river to freeze so men and trucks could cross.

Stalingrad was the turning point in the East. Exhausted German troops surrender.

Early in 1943 Germany only had some 495 tanks on the Russian front. Many more were in Soviet dumps like this one near Stalingrad.

"CITADEL," 1943

Through the winter of 1943, the Russians attacked, wrote Liddell Hart, like a pianist playing the scale. On February 14, they recaptured Rostov on the Don River. The Caucasus armies scampered backwards from another tide line to avoid encirclement. That January, Germany had only 495 battleworthy tanks on the entire front. The Abwehr told Hitler the Russians were making 600 to 700 tanks a month. He slammed a table. "Impossible!" It was not.

The Germans grudgingly fell back against manpower odds up to 6:1. They were even more masterful in retreat than they had been in attack, but Hitler negated this by his insistence his soldiers die where they stood. The Fuhrer's orders so intimidated one officer, he feared "to move my sentry from the window to the door." Russian planes dropped leaflets telling the Germans how to shoot themselves in the foot—a capital offense—without leaving powder burns.

Only the spring thaw stopped the Russians, who could survive on rations that would starve any other soldier. When the ground dried, Hitler rallied his forces for a defensive offensive to wear down the Russians while he waited for where or when the Allies might strike in the West. He massed 2 million men and 3,000 tanks to make a pincer attack on either side of a bulge called the Kursk Salient. This was Operation Citadel which kicked off July 5, 1943. Tanks "scurrying like rats" fought the greatest armored battle of all time. By July 13, the Germans had destroyed 1,800 Russian tanks. But the Red Army, laying up to 40,000 mines in a night, defended itself in depth and Citadel stalled.

On August 4, the Russians, filling their hideous losses with 13-year-olds and even women, counterattacked. Arm-in-arm human waves charged through German mine fields five or six times until they broke out. Zhukov chillingly wrote Eisenhower that the appalling toll would have been as great if they had attacked artillery and machine guns instead of mines. The Russians captured the key city of Orel, held by Germans since the high tide of 1941. In the Ukraine, Hitler, needing men to defend newly-invaded Italy, reluctantly allowed his troops to fall back to the Dnieper River, the last natural barrier before Poland where Barbarossa had begun.

"SYMBOL," 1943

The place: Hotel Anfa, outside Casablanca, January 14-24.

The subject: future strategy.

The players:

George Marshall, in favor of invading France soonest.

Ernest King, for U.S. offensives in the Pacific.

Sir Alan Brooke, for further Allied operations in the Mediterranean, with the hope of enlisting Turkey.

Sir Charles Portal, a peacemaker.

Churchill and Roosevelt, protagonists; De Gaulle, bit player. Stalin, offstage.

Marshall: invade France — Operation Roundup — in 1943 to take pressure off Russia before it collapses. Stalin: refuses a visit by Marshall because of lack of second front. Wedemeyer: U.S. troops still too raw for a major battle. King, given up hard liquor for the duration but not wine, furious the Pacific slighted. British mollify him with promises they have no intention of fulfilling. Some Americans believe Britain secretly hopes Russia and Germany will bleed selves to death, leaving it paramount in Europe. Russia will expand into the Balkans in any event.

Air Marshal Portal describes British, in driver's seat for the last time, as like "a testator who wishes to leave the bulk of his fortune to his mistress. He must, however, leave something to his wife, and his problem is to decide how little he can in decency leave apart for her." U.S. is wife.

Upshot: Roundup scrubbed for 1943, maybe a "go" in 1944. The No. 1 priority: Hitler's U-boats. Then Pointblank, the joint bombing of Germany. Sicily to be invaded — Husky. Troops already in the theater. De Gaulle acknowledges Gen. Henri Giraud, picked by Allies to succeed Darlan, in frostiest handshake of the war.

Curtain call: at news conference concluding Symbol, Roosevelt for first time: the Allies' goal is "unconditional surrender." Churchill: "I wouldn't have used those words." Roosevelt: the thought came to him as he was talking. Actually, had been in his notes, also discussed unofficially.

Intermission: Brooke sees "warblers of all kinds including a white wagtail."

"FLASH"

Gen. Gunther von Kluge thought he and his fellow conspirators had the Fuhrer this time. He had taken the bait by accepting an invitation to fly to Smolensk headquarters March 13, 1943. While there, two Cointreau bottles (they were square and wouldn't roll around) were filled with plastic explosive with an acid wire trigger. The bomb for Operation Flash was set to go off a half-hour after the Fuhrer took off when the plane reached 8,000 feet. The plane encountered turbulence, however. To make his Fuhrer more comfortable, the pilot flew higher. The bomb froze.

In September, another assassination plot went awry. An officer was going to blow up himself and Hitler with a bomb concealed in a new military coat he was demonstrating. But an air raid destroyed all the coats. A second overcoat try was cancelled early in 1944 by another air raid. Gen. Helmuth Stieff also put a bomb in Hitler's Wolf's Lair but lost his nerve before he could explode it. The Grofaz led a charmed life.

German corpses littered the ground after the pivotal Nazi defeat at Stalingrad. Starving troops resorted to cannibalism by the end of the siege.

The city looked, journalist Alexander Werth wrote a few days after the battle, "as though a raving lunatic had suddenly died of heart failure."

Meanwhile, Marshals Konstantin Rokossovky and A.I. Yeremenko had attacked to Paulus's rear, routing the Romanians and taking 30,000 prisoners. On November 22 their two armies met, trapping Paulus and 280,000 Germans in a 20-by-40-mile pocket. Winter descended. The Volga froze December 16. As temperatures fell to -30 degrees centigrade, German soldiers urinated on their weapons to thaw them. Paulus needed 300 tons of supplies a day by airlift. Some days he only got 16. His starving men ate horses, then, as bodies with neatly severed arms attested, their dead.

On December 12, Manstein launched Operation Wintergewitter — Winter Storm — to pry Paulus free. His men got to within 25 miles of Stalingrad, could see its flares at night, but no farther. Sixteen thousand of his soldiers had been killed. He implored Hitler to let Paulus fight his way to him. Hitler refused. He could withdraw only if he held on to Stalingrad. Nor would he let Paulus surrender. "(That) is forbidden. The Sixth Army will hold its positions to the last man and ... make an unforgettable contribution ... toward the salvation of the Western world."

Even Chuikov marvelled at the tenacity of his scarecrow foes. "The Nazis just won't surrender." A German soldier wrote a last letter home: "Of the division there are only 69 men fit for action. All we have are two machine guns and 400 rounds." Knowing that never in German history had a field marshal surrendered, on January 30, 1943, Hitler elevated Paulus to that rank. The next day, Lt. Fyodor Yolchenko captured the new field marshal in the basement of the ruin of a department store. "Well, that finishes it," said the Russian. It did. The Germans surrendered 195,000 men — only 6,000 would survive Russian POW camps to return home — 1,550 tanks, 750 planes, 8,000 cannon and 24 generals.

The Volga remained uncrossed, the most portentous high tide of them all.

"RUDELTAKTIK"

1939-43

Give me 200 submarines, Adm. Karl Doenitz told Hitler before World War II, and I will win the war. He didn't get them. In any event, Doenitz thought he had five years to build a U-boat fleet. He didn't get that, either.

German submarines were a proven weapon. In the first war they almost strangled Great Britain. They almost did again in World War II, but they got a late start. This is baffling, then and now.

Above: *Scourge of the high seas, a German* **Unterseeboot** *or U-boat. More than half of those who served on such vessels were killed in action, the highest percentage of casualties in any service during the war.*

Left: *German submariners watch their victim, a U.S. tanker, sink below the surface of the Atlantic.*

At the time, Air Marshal Sir John Slessor said: "One shudders to think what would have happened if Germany before the war had not been so foolish to build a third-rate heavy ship force at the expense of their really decisive one, the U-boat service."

Much later, in his book "Brute Force" about the strategy and economics of the war, John Ellis writes: "Hitler's mistakes during World War II have filled whole books, but surely the greatest of them was to go to war against a country that depended for its survival upon maritime imports with so feeble a submarine fleet and building program that for the first 15 months it could only average 20 boats at sea in the Atlantic at any one time." Sometimes there were only six.

The Battle of the North Atlantic was the longest of the war, fought for four years the length of the lifeline between democracy's American arsenal and its last toehold in Europe, Great Britain. Fought in winters of 100-mile-an-hour storms and hundred-

Despite such measures as the convoy, the Allies lost more shipping tonnage than they built in 1942. Improved methods of detecting and sinking U-boats and increased ship production caused the tide to turn against the German submariners.

foot seas when ice could capsize a ship, if submarines didn't get there first. Fought off the North Cape of Norway on the Murmansk run where U-boats beneath the sea and bombers above it could nibble away at Russian-bound convoys during the long Arctic days of summer. Fought by fervent young Nazis in rancid, airless tubes that were really submerged cannons. Fought by civilian sailors who could be blown from their bunks one minute, into flaming oil the next, or icy seas that could kill almost at once. It was a battle chronicled by movies such as "The Cruel Sea" and "Das Boot" which cause the viewer to marvel that anyone could fight it.

Versailles forbade Germany to build submarines, a humiliation compounded when the Kaiser's fleet was scuttled at war's end. When Hitler renounced the treaty in 1935, he embarked on a boastful crash program to launch modern, visible surface ships. He did not envision a war of attrition. Bluff had won him Czechoslovakia, blitzkrieg Poland and France. When the war began, Doenitz had only 65 U-boats, most either in maintenance or training. Nonetheless, for submariners it was "Die Gluckliche Zeit" — the Happy Time. On October 13, 1939, U-47 boldly played the currents to sail into Scapa Flow off Scotland to torpedo the battleship Royal Oak right under British noses. Capt. Otto Kretschmer, who sailed with a golden horseshoe on his conning tower, sank 238,000 tons of shipping in 18 months. The Germans had another edge. They had broken British naval codes. As the heavily-laden sheep of

BISMARCK

"What the devil is that?" said an American observer on a British Catalina patrol plane over the Atlantic in May, 1941.

"Looks like a battleship," said the pilot.

It was the Bismarck, Germany's best that had just hit Britain's largest dreadnaught, Hood, May 24, with a direct shot on its magazine. Hood sank in four minutes with only three survivors. After the sighting, ancient, fabric-covered Swordfish biplanes attacked the Bismarck, and one of their torpedoes crippled its steering. Pounded repeatedly from sea and air, the Bismarck was sunk May 27 with almost all of its 2,000-man crew.

the convoys from Sydney and Halifax in Nova Scotia lumbered eastward, the predators of the Rudeltaktik, the wolf packs, gathered to feast on their prey. Even with escorting warships shepherding their flocks, U-boats sank 21 of 30 ships in a convoy in October 1940.

In peacetime, Britain imported 55 million tons of shipping a year. This was soon cut 20 percent and strict rationing imposed. By 1941 when U-boats were sinking 10 percent more tonnage than was being replaced, imports were cut to 32 million tons and belts tightened another notch. The defenses were the escorts; sonar, a form of underwater radar; radio direction finders that located U-boat transmissions back to base and patrol bombers nearer shore. By daringly boarding sinking subs, by a raid on the Lofoten Islands and by dumb luck with a few captures, the British finally broke into the U-boats' Enigma codes.

Before that, the U-boats had target practice off the American East Coast once the United States entered the war. Silhouetted against the lights of resort towns which didn't want to black out the tourists, the unconvoyed, unescorted American freighters were sitting ducks. Bathers in Virginia were horrified to watch a tanker explode right off the beach. Adm. King pigheadedly refused to convoy coastal shipping. Eisenhower confided to his diary: "The war would go more smoothly if King were shot." Killing by this Paukenschlag — Drum Roll— offensive was fueled by "milk cows," submarine supply ships. When King finally took British advice April 3, 1942, and began convoying, the U-boats sailed into the Caribbean. They sank nine tankers in a month coming out of Trinidad.

Doenitz estimated he would win if he could sink 700,000 tons a month, a figure reached May 1942. Next month, 144 Allied ships went down. Sailors nervously lived on coffee and guts and raced for the nearest companionway if someone dropped a wrench or sneezed too loudly.

Doenitz had ordered all submariners to send a code word in letters home if they were captured and thought Enigma had been compromised, so the escorts hustled prisoners below whenever they boarded a crippled U-boat.

It was becoming a battle between American and British shipyards and the torpedoes. In 1942, the Allies launched 7.39 million tons, but lost 7.78 mil-

Left: *By mid-1943 the Battle of the Atlantic had been won with the help of radar, code-breaking, long-range bombers and improved convoys. Only the rare U-boat ventured into the vital sea lanes to suffer the fate of this German submarine sunk by a British patrol bomber.*

lion. But in 1943 with production in full swing, they built 15.45 million tons. Using prefabricated sections, Henry Kaiser's West Coast yard laid the keel of the Liberty Ship Robert E. Peary and launched the completed vessel four days and 15 hours later. Britain got delivery of the first of six 30-plane escort carriers seven months after the order was placed.

The killing went on. Convoy PQ17 carrying Lend-Lease supplies to Murmansk lost 22 of 33 ships in an air-sea attack in July 1942. In September eight ships of PQ18 were sunk in eight minutes.

But the edge was shifting. Patrol plane radar could pick up U-boats as they surfaced to get a breath of fresh air and charge batteries. If they couldn't depth-charge the U-boats, they at least forced them to submerge where their speed dropped from 19 knots to eight, even slower than the slowest merchantmen. Germany then developed a radar detector. The Allies came up with a narrower beam radar the U-boats couldn't detect. Convoy escorts were beefed up with the escort carriers and corvettes and destroyer escorts. The United States turned out 10 DEs a month. Canada, a major player, began the war with 17 warships. It ended it with 378. Bomber Command had resisted giving long-range bombers to the North Atlantic campaign but grudgingly released Amercan-made B-24s which had twice the range. The "Greenland Gap," where the wolf packs used to be immune from the air, was no more.

Notwithstanding, in March 1943 the U-boats set a record: 82 ships. But in May, the Germans lost 43 submarines. Doenitz suspected Enigma had been broken. "Out of the question," said investigators. Anyway Doenitz called off the wolves from the North Atlantic May 24. They came back in the fall. Planes sank 23 submarines in six weeks. One was a milk cow, U-459, sunk when W.H.T. Jennings flew his crippled Wellington bomber into her conning tower. (Only one of 17 milk cows survived the war.) By October the Allies shipyards had replaced all the tonnage lost in the war. A tide had turned again.

Early in 1944, Doenitz finally vacated the North Atlantic after losing 36 U-boats in the first three months of the year. Only a few weather subs remained. The North Atlantic had become a milk run. In January-March 1944, only three ships of 3,360 convoyed were lost.

Of 40,900 German submariners, 25,870 died, including two sons of Doenitz, the highest percentage of any service of any combatant. They had sunk 2,828 ships totalling 14,687,231 tons. Thirty-two thousand British seamen — a quarter of all who served — died, plus 6,000 Americans. In time, their Atlantic graveyard purged itself of the flaming and choking oil slicks, the empty life rafts, the floating hatch covers and bodies and only the sea remained to mark the battle. Not a cruel sea. Just indifferent.

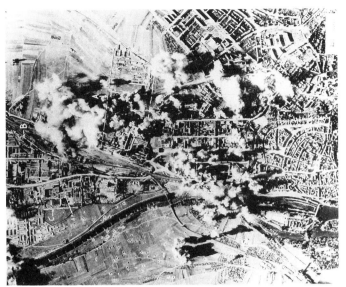

"POINTBLANK"

1939-45

The day World War II began, Roosevelt appealed to the belligerents not to bomb civilians. Britain, France and Germany quickly agreed not to.

Four days later, Air Minister Kingsley Wood was asked by the RAF to authorize bombing German

Above: The U.S. raid on the ball-bearing works at Schweinfurt cost an appalling 60 bombers. It crippled production temporarily and could have done so permanently if the raids had persisted, Germans said after the war.

Left: The heroic raid by American B-24 Liberators on the Ploesti oil fields in Romania came in so low some propellers were slicing sunflowers. Fifty-nine of 178 bombers were lost, five crewmen won Medals of Honor — but the refineries were soon back at full production.

ammo dumps by setting the bone-dry Black Forest on fire. Wood refused. It would destroy "private property," he reasoned.

Also early in the war, the pilot of a German Heinkel bomber crashed to his death near an English village. He was buried in the local cemetery with full military honors.

None of this gentility endured.

For some reason, air war had a tinge of chivalry to it. In the first war, enemy pilots used to wave and salute each other. Dogfights and the Red Barons came later. Zeppelins bombed London a few times as did huge orange-crate German bombers. But turning the sky into a battleground seemed a rape of the empyrean. It also meant for civilians the front lines were no farther away than a bomb in the bedroom.

The Japanese had no qualms about bombing Shanghai indiscriminately in 1937, the same year German Heinkels and Junkers fighting for Francisco

Daylight precision bombing raids of B-17s such as pictured here took heavy casualties.

Franco in the Spanish Civil War killed 1,654 civilians in the sacred Basque town of Guernica in what Goering later admitted was a "test." The results must have satisfied the Deputy Reichsfuhrer because as soon as war began Stukas with their screaming sirens terror-bombed Polish villages far from battle while bigger bombers plastered Warsaw. Roosevelt had been whistling in the wind. People were now a prime target: their morale, their homes, where they worked. Civilians: military objectives. Some 146,777 Britons were casualties of bombing in the war, 500,000 to 600,000 German civilians died and probably more Japanese. Total war had engendered a ferocious barbarity.

"TRIDENT"
1943

Scene: Washington, May 1943.

Players: Churchill, Roosevelt, Brooke, Marshall et al.

Prologue: Prime Minister sails over on Queen Mary along with load of Italian POWs.

Plot: Brooke says Britain won't be ready to invade France until 1945 or 1946. Churchill is for invasion of Italy after Husky invades Sicily to "chill" German people. Marshall: Italy would delay fighting Japan, "which is not acceptable to us." Threatens to go all out in the Pacific if no European landing in 1944. A bluff.

Denouement: European invasion scheduled for May 1, 1944, with twenty nine divisions. Italy to be invaded but only enough to bring its surrender. By November 1, 1943, seven divisions to be transferred from Italy to England for D-Day.

Subplots: Marshall brilliantly keeps peace between the U.S. and U.K., U.S. Army and U.S. Army Air Force, U.S. Army Air Force and U.S. Navy, and U.S. Navy and Douglas MacArthur.

Intermission: Spring break for all at Colonial Williamsburg, Virginia. Marshall almost exhausts musical repertoire playing "Poor Butterfly" on spinet. Brooke bird-watches, spies robin, visits site of earlier Anglo-American collaboration at Yorktown which, in view former colonial offspring now supporting Mother Country, one Englishman calls "Britain's greatest victory."

"We're drowning and burning Japs all over the Pacific," said Adm. William "Bull" Halsey, "and it is just as much pleasure to burn them as to drown them."

Initial British raids were in daylight against specific targets. Heavy casualties soon led the RAF Bomber Command under Air Marshal Sir Arthur "Bomber" Harris to switch to area bombing at night. At first the RAF lost more airmen than were killed on the ground. Night bombing was so haphazard that a 1942 RAF survey said less than 25 percent of the bombs fell in urban areas, most missing by more than five miles. "We made a major assault on German agriculture," said a pilot. Furthermore, the U.S. Strategic Bombing Survey after the war found that 14 percent of the bombs didn't even explode.

The use of pathfinder bombers to outline targets with colored incendiary bombs turned the city of Hamburg into a pyre with hurricane-force winds funneling into the 1,800-degree inferno and spreading the blaze. Authorities guessed 20,000 people died, but could not be sure. Many were just ashes. A point to remember is that within five months production in Hamburg was back to 80 percent of normal.

The American approach was different: to bomb precisely by day relying on the hush-hush Norden bombsight. The massed machine guns from a B-17 group could spit out 18 tons of bullets a minute. Commanded by Maj. Gen. Carl "Tooey" Spaatz, said to look "like a rusty nail," the 8th Air Force's first attack was on Rouen in France August 17, 1942. It was a modest strike compared to the RAF's first thousand-bomber raid that May on Cologne. The RAF calculated bombs on U.S. daylight raids hit within 450 yards in good weather, 1,200 yards in poor. At night RAF bombs fell within a three-mile radius.

It was a young man's war led by commanders who had a messianic belief that bombing would win the war. "Give me 20,000 bombers and I will finish Germany in a week," said Harris. It took a young man's nerves to stay on course while the bombardier fine-tuned his sight on the final approach. And it took the insouciance of youth to face the empty chairs at table that night at dinner.

Men of the wild blue yonder figured themselves an elite corps. Pilots needed a college degree. Robert A. Lovett, a World War I flier, Wall Street investment banker and as assistant secretary of war for air the brains behind Gen. Henry H. "Hap" Arnold, the Army's ranking airman, tried the flight entrance test along with the president of MIT. Both failed. (The highest grade among MIT students was "a young girl from Flatbush whose family were a bunch of musicians.")

The first Army Air Corps — later Army Air Forces — B-17 landed in Prestwick, Scotland, July 1, 1942. The day-night, American-Anglo Pointblank was dominated at first by RAF "city-busting" raids. But the most dramatic raid of the war occurred August 1, 1943, by 178 U.S. B-24s from Libya bearing names like "Vulgar Virgin" and "Old Baldy" and "Li'l Joe" on the Romanian oil refineries at Ploesti. Ploesti was the heartbeat of Hitler's war machine, producing 400,000 tons of fuel a year. Flying so low the propellers of some of the planes sliced through sunflowers, 140 bombers reached the target in a heroic attack that won five Medals of Honor, three posthumous. But 59 of the American planes were shot down or crashed, and 450 airmen were killed or missing. "To think that last year at this time I was working in a gas station," said a survivor. But within weeks Ploesti was producing more fuel than ever.

Worse were two raids August 17 and October 14, 1943, on Germany's crucial ball-bearing complex at Schweinfurt. A total of 120 B-17s were shot down of 667, and in the second raid 22 damaged beyond repair. Col. Curtis LeMay had devised a box formation to maximize the Flying Fortresses' firepower and minimize loss, but flying without fighter cover had proven to be seven times more costly than with it. The United States put strategic bombing on hold. That was the dilemma. Hitler's production czar, Albert Speer, estimated the first raid cut Germany's irreplaceable ball bearing output by 38 percent, the second raid 67 percent. A follow-up raid might have halted production, but the cost was too great. Speer was able to decentralize the factories.

The B-17 was a remarkably durable plane. One pilot made it home seven times in 'Forts that were almost total wrecks. He named them all "Hang the Expense." In the 379th Bomb Group, B-17 "Tondelayo," Dorothy Lamour's film name in a sarong epic, landed in England with 11 cannon shells in its fuel tanks. (They were all duds. Explosives people opened them up to find out why. Inside one was a note in Czech from the assembly line: "This is all we can do for you now.")

The Allies were winning the air battle on the factory ground. In June 1942, Germany had only 68 more planes than a year earlier. In 1943 the U.S. produced 85,898 aircraft, the other Allies another 15,741 to only 18,953 for Germany. The next year it was Allies 125,718, Germany 33,804. The combat ratios were 5:1, then 9:1 respectively. The key ingredient was the whale-bodied P-47 — the "Jug" — which could escort bombers all the way to the target because of a simple invention: jettisonable wing tanks. In mid-1944, the Jug was joined by the plane many called the war's best piston-engined fighter, the Merlin-powered P-51 Mustang, built from drawing board to prototype in just over 100 days. In one week in 1944 Americans claimed 600 German fighters downed. Adolf Galland, the Luftwaffe fighter chief, said his losses were 50 planes per Allied raid. Pointblank had resumed in 1944 with a parade of bombers over increasingly defenseless Germany. The Luftwaffe dropped 30,000 tons on London during the Blitz. In just five months in 1944 the Allies rained 600,000 tons of bombs on the Third Reich. What it all proved is yet to be settled.

John Ellis in his book calls Harris's area bombing "one of the most dubious policies, both militarily and morally." In his book "The Second World War," Maj. Gen. J.F.C. Fuller writes that bombing was "a war of devastation and terrorization unrivalled since the invasion of the Seljuks." And also: "a grotesque failure."

Despite the barrage, German production actually reached a peak in July 1944. But between April and September, German output of synthetic fuel was reduced from 348,000 tons to 26,000, aviation fuel from 175,000 tons to 17,000. Horses had to drag fighters to takeoff. But, the U.S. Strategic Bombing Survey said, the bombers did not "persevere to the kill."

In preparation for D-Day, the bombers attacked Germany's transport system relentlessly. Field Marshal Albert Kesselring, a former Luftwaffe commander later to lead German troops in Italy, said after the war: "Your air force decided the conflict (by) destruction of the transport system." Railroad loadings were 829,000 the week of August 12, 1944 and only 214,000 the week ending March 3, 1945. By February 1945, said the USSBS, "except in limited

Airplane assembly line. A flock of B-24 Liberators under construction at a Consolidated Aircraft Corporation plant in Texas.

areas the coal supply had been eliminated ... Orderly production was no longer possible." "Nazi Germany was no longer an industrial nation," concluded an Air Force historian.

However, the bombers ignored a major target: Germany's electrical grid. One hundred generating plants provided 56.3 percent of Germany's power. If only five had been destroyed, German power would have been cut 8 percent. One German said if only one of Berlin's utility plants had been destroyed, the city would have been as dead as after months of bombing. This after a death rate of 47.5 percent among Bomber Command crews for the war.

But the bombing had secondary benefits. Germany had to drain its resources to make fighters, to use 88s as anti-aircraft guns instead of frontline artillery in Russia or Normandy. A third of the country's electronics and optic industry was preoccupied making radars and gunsights.

Back in America, Rosie the Riveters kept banging

JETS

German aircraft designers were great tinkerers. While Britain focused on its Spitfires and Hurricanes, Messerschmitt designers were playing around with forty different concepts and almost as many prototypes.

Hitler loved "secret weapons" and trusted them to win the war even at the last hour. The V-1 and V-2 rockets were terror weapons, but the ME-262 was the world's first jet. It could fly rings around anything in the sky. It arrived too late in the war, however, to be decisive, and Hitler foolishly insisted it be used as a fighter-bomber, not an interceptor.

out bombers, but George Marshall maintained the war must be won on the ground. This was so.

16

"HUSKY"

1943

To the Americans, the invasion of Sicily was castor oil. They took it because the British said it would be good for them. They would much rather have been in England practicing to invade France.

To 200,000 Italian soldiers, it was *troppo* — too much. They were fed up with a war that wouldn't even supply them with field kitchens while their

Above: The U.S. Seventh Army hit the beaches in Sicily without too much difficulty, but the accompanying airdrop scattered paratroopers over hundreds of square miles.

Left: Mussolini vowed he'd throw the invaders of Sicily into the sea at the beaches. Not here, where the British Eighth Army came ashore. Real fighting began inland.

officers feasted every night. The only good thing was that they hardly ever visited the troops.

"It was a curious position," wrote journalist Romano Giachetti. "Men still armed were forced to fire at an enemy that was actually their friend. The enemy was among them: Fascists and Germans."

The Italian attitude was demonstrated June 11 when 11,000 Italians surrendered the steppingstone island of Pantelleria between Tunisia and Sicily before a British invasion force could even land. The only casualty was a Tommy bitten by a mule.

D-Day for Sicily was July 10 when 10 Allied divisions under Eisenhower's deputy, Sir Harold Alexander, came ashore. The Anglo-American force consisted of Montgomery and the Eighth Army and the American Seventh Army under Patton with Bradley as a corps commander. Said he: "Seldom in war has a major operation been undertaken in such a fog of indecision, confusion and conflicting plans."

For starters, 23 planes carrying the 82nd Airborne

Division were shot down by U.S. Navy gunners with a loss of 229 men. The rest of the paratroopers were scattered all over the countryside. Once the men were ashore off newly-designed landing craft including the 328-foot Landing Ship Tank — LSTs, informally called Large Stationary Targets — there were no definitive plans. Montgomery, true to his fashion, built up his forces before attacking north to Messina. To the west, Patton chafed at routinely safeguarding Monty's left flank.

The Italians were no less confused. Right after landing, Mike Chinigo of the International News Service picked up a phone that was ringing in a captured Italian bunker. An Italian general asked if an invasion was going on. "Say it isn't so!" he exclaimed. It wasn't so, said Chinigo, who spoke Italian. The satisfied general hung up. A Brit found he couldn't fire his machine gun at the Germans for the surrendering Italians trying to give up to him. "Get lost!" he screamed. Just so there wouldn't be any tricks, GIs took their POWs' belts and cut off their fly buttons so the Italians had to keep hands busy holding up their pants.

While Montgomery finally attacked in heavy fighting, Patton sped off in search of publicity and Palermo at the west end of the island. He got both, remarking: "The Allies must fight in separate theaters, or they hate each other more than they do the enemy." Eisenhower was as put off by Patton's blitz as he was by Montgomery's set-piece tactics. His naval commander, Adm. Sir Andrew Cunningham, wouldn't even allow his countryman's name mentioned in his presence. "In dealing with (Monty)," said another Briton, "one must remember that he isn't quite a gentleman."

Along with Patton, the 3rd Division of Maj. Gen. Lucian Truscott showed American mobility by marching 100 miles in the heat in three days. This was the "Truscott Trot," a five-mile-an-hour pace, twice the standard. But nobody could get to Messina in time to stop the Germans from staging a Dunkirk

The ivory-handled .45, the cavalry boots, the swagger stick. They were all part of Lt. Gen. George S. Patton, a profane esthete who commanded the U.S. forces in Sicily but almost got fired from the war for accusing two G.I.s of cowardice and slapping them.

of their own. After holding off 450,000 Allied soldiers for 38 days, 60,000 Germans were ferried a mile across the Straits of Messina to the boot of Italy. The Germans boldly evacuated even at high noon knowing Allied pilots habitually broke for lunch.

Patton's glory was short-lived. On August 3 he visited a field hospital and slapped Pvt. Charles Kuhl of Mishawaka, Wisconsin, for "shirking." "One sometimes slaps a baby to bring it to," Patton excused himself in his diary. Two days later he waved one of his ivory-handled Colts at Pvt. Paul Bennett in a hospital: "I ought to shoot you myself right now, God damn you!" he shouted. Eisenhower insisted Patton apologize to all his men before relieving him. Several divisions applauded him. Then he addressed the men of the 1st Division, the Army's oldest, in the ruins of a Roman amphitheater. First he warned the soldiers against consorting with Italian women, "a dirty, diseased people." At the end, he said he was obeying an order to apologize and did so. He was greeted by silence. As he left, boos were heard from the now veteran troops.

"QUADRANT" 1943

Summit conference Quebec, August 14-24, 1943.

Cast: usual suspects including FDR (code name Admiral Q, also Victor), Churchill (Former Naval Person, also Colonel Warden), Marshall (Braid).

Landing in Italy, Avalanche, approved. Overlord, landing in France, set for May 1, 1944, although Former Naval Person sets generals' teeth on edge with will-o'-the-wisp schemes to invade Norway (Jupiter) or Yugoslav Dalmatian coast and on into Balkans; any place but France. He is haunted by memories of World War I carnage. New fight looms: whether to invade southern France in addition to Normandy. Admiral Q wants American to lead Overlord. Eventually it will be Duckpin (Eisenhower).

Churchill, late late night owl, chivies Maj. Gen. Sir Hastings Ismay, his much-decorated personal chief of staff, who is up past bedtime: "There you stand loaded down with honors by your country, and now you betray her. Go to bed if you like, but I expect to do my duty."

Sicily was a sweltering, dusty, sometimes gallop, sometimes deadly learning ground for America's citizen army.

Meanwhile, on July 24, the Fascist Grand Council met in Rome for the first time in three-and-a-half years to pass judgment on Mussolini. Il Duce had vowed to throw the Allies back into the sea from Sicily "right at the water's edge." Instead, by a vote of 19-2, the council threw him out. "Il gioco e finito," King Victor Emmanuel told him. The game is over. "Salute the Duce!" an aide cried to the council. "No," said the departing dictator, "I excuse you from that."

Right: Patton won the race with Britain's Montgomery to capture Messina in Sicily first. But in a masterful evacuation, plus Allied blunders, the Germans got away.

He was arrested, then rescued by Hitler's commando daredevil, Col. Otto Skorzeny, and played out the rest of the war as Hitler's puppet.

17

"AVALANCHE"

1943-44

Winston Churchill had a fascination for soft underbellies (his term). It was an old British tradition. Cornwallis tried to end the American Revolution from the Carolinas. Wellington had at Napoleon via Spain. Churchill himself in World War I had fathered the disastrous Gallipoli campaign to strike the Kaiser through Turkey. But he, a historian, should have known. Only once in the ancient his-

Above: *The first Americans to set foot on the European continent came ashore at Salerno south of Naples. Twenty-one months of fighting lay ahead.*

Left: *The Salerno landing was almost thrown off the beach, but the GIs and their Allies grudgingly fought upon some of the war's worst terrain to become only the second army in history to capture Rome from the south.*

tory of the Italian peninsula had a conquerer taken Rome from the south. But, the Prime Minister confidently predicted, the Allies would ascend the Italian boot "like bugs up a trouser leg."

The Italian campaign, starting with Avalanche, a landing at Salerno, and Buttress, the 8th Army coming ashore at the toe of the boot, would theoretically suck in German divisions from Russia and Normandy. Suck in men and materiel better employed in France, muttered the Americans.

Both were right.

Alan Brooke came away from Trident convinced, correctly, that the Americans believed Britain was "leading them down the garden path" with further campaigns in the Mediterranean. The Yanks saw a dissipation of energy from the second front Roosevelt kept promising Stalin. Landing craft were short. Occupying Italy would require, for starters, importing 10 million tons of coal to warm the natives. Churchill flew to woo Eisenhower with

WILLIE & JOE

Nobody put a finger on the mud, the mountains, the blood of Italy better than 22-year-old cartoonist Sgt. Bill Mauldin and aching back columnist Ernie Pyle. Both won Pulitzers by wiping away any glamour of war and telling it like it was, a war of the Common Man fighting the Germans, the odds, the cold and rear-echelon idiocy.

Mauldin's bewhiskered, bedraggled GIs, Willie and Joe, outraged Patton, the war lover, but they became metaphors for World War II. Churchill noted that the Americans thought they had been led down a garden path "but what a beautiful path it has proved to be. They have picked peaches here, nectarines there. How grateful they should be," he said in military similes. The only beauty in Pyle and Mauldin was the beauty of truth.

Sgt. Bill Mauldin's sardonic cartoons deglorified war by depicting mud and blood from the front.

Field Marshal Albert Kesselring made the Allies fight desperately for gains in the rough terrain of Italy.

eloquence over midnight brandies. He succeeded. Meanwhile, in neutral Lisbon, the Italians secretly negotiated surrender terms with the Allies, leaving the Germans potentially between a hard place and a rock, which most of the upcoming battleground was, should their former Axis partners turn on them. On September 7, 1943, Brig. Gen. Maxwell Taylor stole into Rome to determine if the 82nd Airborne could take the city with an air drop. His hosts exaggerated German strength. It took, in fact, two days for the Nazis to retake the Eternal City from the Italians when they officially left the war September 8. The next day the Allied 5th Army, led by 49-year-old Lt. Gen. Mark Clark, landed at Salerno. By nightfall the 36th Division, a Texan National Guard unit, had pushed four miles inland. They were the first Americans ashore on the European mainland.

On the beach, quartermasters struggled to unload the LSTs, crammed as willy-nilly as a woman's purse. There was even a piano for a sergeants mess-to-come. British Commandos, led by Col.

Allied operations for 1943. While Russia forced the Nazis back on the Eastern front, the rest of the Allies under the U.S. and Britain invaded Italy through Sicily while an invasion was threatened on the coast of France.

"Mad Jack" Churchill who went into battle with his bagpiper and a claymore, the fighting sword of his Scots ancestors, captured their assigned objectives at the base of the Amalfi peninsula.

German reinforcements rushed to the beachhead, and on the 13th, Kesselring, the one-time Luftwaffe general, counterattacked and almost drove between the Allies to the sea. Cooks, orderlies, anybody grabbed rifles. Clark debated whether to move his headquarters offshore. The 155 mm howitzers were firing point blank. A GI in a barn banged mortar shells on the floor, then tossed them like grenades at the Germans. Bombers and warships raked the

Germans, and the 82nd made a drop. The toehold held, and prisoners started coming in. Pvt. Ike Franklin, conversely, had been captured by the Germans along with some plasma bottles. The Germans refused to use it for their wounded. "Our orders are clear," said an enemy physician. "It might be Jewish or Negro blood."

Clark eagerly awaited the arrival of Montgomery from the south where he had only made 45 miles in a week against little opposition. "I have not been told of any plan," Monty explained, "and I must therefore assume that there was none." Clark was to say: "(Montgomery) landed first, and he was coming up, well, I won't say leisurely, but it sure wasn't as fast as I had hoped. I kept getting messages, 'Hold up, we've joined hands.' I sent a message back: 'If we've joined hands, I haven't felt a thing yet.'"

The two armies linked up September 17, and Kesselring fell back. His successful defense, however, persuaded Hitler, against Rommel's advice, to withdraw to a defense line in northern Italy, to fight for every inch. Plainly this was not to be North Africa where, an Army historian admits, "we needed a place to be lousy in." The untried Americans had passed their first test. "We just thought that was the way war was, and we didn't know any better. If we had known better, we might not have made it," said a GI.

Naples fell October 1 and Foggia with its airfields to the east October 11. These, writes Gen. Fuller, were "reasonable" goals. Rome was a "political" one. Anything north of there was "daft." But by mid-October, Hitler had poured in nine more divisions than the Allies had. Churchill's strategy had worked. But who was stalemating whom was moot. Instead of training for France, 1 million Allied men were bogged down in the most miserable campaign of the war.

Of Naples, correspondent Alan Moorehead wrote: "In the whole list of sordid human vices, none, I think, were overlooked in Naples." As many as 70 Army vehicles were stolen a night. Ten-year-olds staffed brothels. GIs went blind on poisoned brandy. The departing Nazis scuttled 130 ships in the harbor. But the Army Engineers had the port operative in three days. The troops moved out into the mountains, every one a potential fort among the rocks. "God's gift to gunners," Kesselring described the Appenines. Portable pillboxes of steel five inches thick were moved to the heights. Everywhere, Germans planted mines: mines that blew off a foot at a tip-toe touch, mines that jumped up and exploded at waist height, severing legs, mines that blew treads off tanks.

The attackers had a choice: advance up the few valleys into the sights of the 88s or claw tooth and nail through the mountains. The Allies did both.

"The Americans kept sending tanks down the road," said a German artillery officer. "We kept knocking them out. Finally, we would run out of

---

"SEXTANT/EUREKA" 1943

Scene: double feature Summit: Cairo (Sextant) November 22-26, then Tehran (Eureka) November 28-December 1.

Cast: usual plus Chiang Kai-shek (code name Celestes, also Peanut) at Sextant, Stalin (Glyptic) at Eureka.

Churchill on Sino-Japanese war: "Lengthy, complicated and minor." At Cairo, Adm. King so mad at Brooke, who wants to cancel Burma invasion and use landing craft in Mediterranean, he almost jumps over table at him. "Vinegar Joe" Stilwell: "God, was he mad. I wish he had socked him."

Dill, peacemaker, to Brooke: "The American chiefs of staff have given way to our views a thousand more times than we have to theirs."

Churchill: let's invade Rhodes. Marshall: "Not one American is going to die on that goddamn beach!"

Marshall on Glyptic: "I always thought (the British) made a mistake of treating Stalin as if he were a product of the Foreign Service. He was a rough SOB who made his way by murder and should be talked to that way."

Stalin all for invading Normandy, plus landing in southern France (Anvil, later Dragoon which less revealing name) afterwards. British vehemently opposed to Anvil: would weaken Italian campaign, prevent Balkan invasion. Churchill angry, will threaten to resign, but no longer senior partner. D-Day in May 1944 reaffirmed.

On way to Cairo, Roosevelt tells Eisenhower no one remembers Henry Halleck, Union chief of staff in Civil War. Remember Grant and Lee instead. "George Marshall is entitled to his place in history as a great general" by commanding French invasion. On way home, Marshall too proud and too much a soldier to ask for job, so President names Ike. Roosevelt: "I'll sleep better" knowing Marshall chief of staff. Churchill calls him, rightly, "the architect of victory."

Cassino was a metaphor for the fighting in Italy where savage combat went room to room in the rubble.

ammunition. The Americans didn't run out of tanks. That's it in a nutshell."

Mines were everywhere. Duncan Noble, an ambulance driver with the American Field Service, once had four wounded in the back. They had six limbs among them.

High in the mountains, men cowered among the rocks, lethal as shrapnel when shells splintered them. They waited for darkness to relieve themselves. Snipers would get them literally with their pants down by day. Sometimes the enemies were so close they threw rocks or their slops at each other. Men huddled three to a hole filled with icy water in the sleet, snow and rain that made sunny Italy a cruel joke.

A rush call went out back in the States for mules and mule skinners. Of one supply train of 30 pack

mules, snipers got 28. When even mules couldn't make it, men took over hand by hand. Some men were up there a month without a hot meal. "They lived like men of prehistoric times," wrote Ernie Pyle, "and a club would have become them more than a machine gun."

The terrain did not invite ingenuity and got none. An example was the attack the night of January 20, 1944, by the 36th across the frigid Rapido River into the very barrels of German guns. "I never saw any make it to the other side," said Hughes Rudd, later a television newsman, then an artillery spotter in a Piper Cub. "I had 184 men," said an outraged major. "Forty-eight hours later I had 17. If that's not mass murder, I don't know what is." A sergeant remembered: "It was the only scene I'd seen in the war that lived up to what you see in the movies. I had never

seen so many bodies. I remember this kid being hit by a machine gun: the bullets hitting him pushed his body along like a tin can." A congressional hearing was to clear Clark and his staff for ordering the repeated assault, but the Texans did not.

On January 22, the Americans tried an end run, Operation Shingle, a landing up the Tyhrrenian seacoast behind Germany's Gustav Line. Eisenhower was convinced four divisions would be needed, but British intelligence said two would suffice. "I felt like a lamb being led to slaughter," said Ike. The landing commander, Maj. Gen. John P. Lucas, predicted: "They will end up putting me ashore with inadequate forces and get me in a serious jam. Then who will take the blame?" He did when the troops did, indeed, surprise Kesselring and had a clear shot to Rome but secured the beachhead instead. Now there were two stalemates. And Monte Cassino.

The abrupt face of the mountain glowered 1,500 feet above the Liri Valley. At its top was the great monastery first built by St. Benedict in 529 and sacked twice since. The mount was defended by Lt. Gen. Frido von Senger und Etterlin, ironically a Benedictine layman and Rhodes Scholar, hater of Hitler and man of honor. When he had Christmas dinner with the monks, he didn't look out the windows to spot American positions lest he compromise the monks' neutrality.

Three times the Allies tried to capture the height, first with the 34th Division which got to within 400 yards of the top. Then, after the monastery was obliterated by bombing February 15, Indians with two regiments of the splendid Gurkhas from Nepal, tried. And New Zealanders. And Poles. None made it. Meanwhile, down in what remained of the town, a German Tiger tank turned the lobby of the Continental Hotel into a fortress while Americans and Germans machine-gunned each other up and down the stairways. Alexander, who at Dunkirk wryly said surrender might be a good idea, "but I don't know the form for surrendering, so we can't," paid the Germans tribute: "I doubt if there are any other troops in the world who could have stood up to it

The American landing at Anzio was planned to end the stalemate in the mountains of Italy. Instead, it produced another one.

and then gone on fighting with the ferocity they have." John Ellis wrote: "The campaign must rank as one of the greatest defensive achievements in the history of war."

Ernie Pyle described the landscape in the valleys between the mountains of death: "... the limb of an olive tree broken off; six swollen dead horses in the corner of a field, a strawstack burned down; little gray patches of powder burns on the hillside; snatches of broken and abandoned rifles and grenades in the bushes; grain fields patterned with a million criss-crossing ruts from great trucks crawling frame-deep through the mud; empty gun pits and countless foxholes and rubbish-heap stacks of empty C-ration cans and now and then the lone grave of a German soldier."

By now the 5th Army was a motley of Poles, Senegalese, South Africans, Canadians, Brazilians, Mauritians, Yugoslavs, Algerians, Basutos, even some Italians. The Moroccan goumiers were in their element. By day they lovingly honed their knives. An officer asked one to find him a German wrist watch. The goumier obliged that night, presenting the booty with the arm still attached.

In May, spring arrived. Poppies bloomed. Nightingales sang between shell bursts. The Allies moved forward. On May 25, Capt. Ben Souza, leading a patrol out of Anzio, encountered an American engineer lieutenant inspecting a bridge. "Where the hell do you think you're going?" Souza demanded. "I'm trying to make contact with Anzio," the officer replied. "Boy, you've made it!"

Other troops fought up the Liri Valley, the old Roman Via Casilina. "Always and everywhere the procedure and pattern were the same," wrote young correspondent Eric Sevareid. "German guns betrayed their presence. We called our planes to bomb them. Then we concentrated our artillery, too numerous to be opposed. Thereupon, the infantry flowed slowly ahead ... The news would go out to the world that the place was 'liberated.' This is the way it was, day after day, town after town."

In some German divisions, only 400 men were fit for fighting. Enemy planes circled overhead in "cab parks" waiting to be called in to attack. But Kesselring wasn't beaten. He outthought his opponents, gradually pivoting his army inland, leaving the road to Rome open but saving his men from encirclement.

Sherman tanks arrive on the Anzio beachhead.

In Rome an American nun described the flight of "wild-eyed, unshaven, unkempt (men) on foot, in stolen cars, in horse-drawn vehicles, even carts belonging to the street cleaning department ... handsome motor cars with Fascist dignitaries looking anything but dignified in their anxiety to get away ... They were frightened."

Clark was desperate to get to Rome before the Normandy invasion stole the headlines. He scheduled a photo opportunity entering the Eternal City for 4 p.m. June 4. But there were still some Germans with fight left. "Tell the general to give me an hour," said Maj. Gen. Geoffrey Keyes of the U.S. II Corps.

Clark got his picture. The Allies got the first Axis capital to fall. Behind were 20,389 Allied dead, 11,292 of them American, who lay with the many who had failed to take Rome from the south. But the living Willies and Joes had.

Photo opportunity of a life time. Lt. Gen. Mark Clark triumphantly enters Rome.

18

"OVERLORD"

1944

The first GI foot to step ashore in the United Kingdom belonged to Pfc. Melburn Henke. The date was January 26, 1942. Two million Americans were to follow him. The peaceful invasion turned southern England into a vast military encampment as Yanks settled in among villages such as Straight Stolley, Crooked Stolley, Ogbourne St. George and Mildenhall, pronounced "Minal," mind ye. They learned about warm beer and darts and

Above: *On the eve of D-Day, Churchill reviews some GIs, their identifying shoulder patches blotted out by the censor.*

Left: *Supreme Allied Commander Eisenhower chats with U.S. paratroopers shortly before making the toughest decision of the war in Europe: invade France or postpone because of bad weather.*

British reserve and withstood jokes that they were "overpaid and oversexed and over here."

Ever since March 12, 1943, British Lt. Gen. Sir Frederick Morgan had been planning the invasion as Chief of Staff to the Supreme Allied Commander (COSSAC). Normandy, with its shelving beaches, was selected early on. The bluffs of Dieppe had shown that the shortest route from Dover to the Pas-de-Calais was the longest way 'round. But in one of the most elaborate, clever and successful campaigns of disinformation ever, the Allies tried to delude the Germans into thinking just the opposite. Hitler's "instinct" told him Normandy would be the target, but he kept the bulk of his 78 divisions of western Europe in the Pas-de-Calais.

Brooke told Morgan: "It won't work, but you must bloody well make it." Marshall had risen in Brooke's estimation and vice versa, but Eisenhower, now Commander, Supreme Headquarters Allied Expeditionary Force (SHAEF), he thought was "just a coordinator, a good mixer, a champion of inter-Allied cooperation, and in those respects few can hold a candle to him. But is that enough?" Omar Bradley thought his old classmate "had matured into a charming man with a first class mind." True, Ike read pulp Westerns "because I don't have to think." But, said one colleague, "few who watched him carefully indulged the fantasy that he was a genial, open, barefoot boy from Abilene who just happened to be in the right place when lightning struck." He sent an American general home not because he called an Englishman a son-of-a-bitch but because "you called him a limey son-of-a-bitch."

Bradley, who was to lead the Americans, "might have passed as an elderly rifleman," said a correspondent. He was "the least dressed-up commander of an American army since Zachary Taylor, and he wore a straw hat," wrote A.J. Liebling of The New Yorker. But, in his little black book, Marshall had noted: "Quiet, unassuming, capable, sound common sense. Absolute dependabiltiy. Give him a job and forget it."

Overall command of the landing force was given to Montgomery — "God Almonty," to some. "We never lost confidence in him," said an aide, "but we would very often say, 'Oh, Christ, what's the little bugger doing now?!'" Brooke confided to King George VI he "was a very good soldier, but I think he's after my job." "I thought he was after mine," the King replied.

Wags said the only thing that kept Britain from sinking were the tethered barrage balloons. Crammed into the country lanes and thatched cottages besides the Americans were 1.75 million British and Commonwealth troops plus 40,000 French, Poles, Norwegians and Belgians. Each armored division needed 40 shiploads to supply it, an infantry division 30. Fields were stacked with shells, manor houses and schools with men. By April 1944, half a million tons were landing monthly. The United States alone stocked 700,000 separate items: 8,000 planes, 1,000 locomotives, 100,000 packs of gum with 54,000 men just to keep track of it all. Men filled 279,000 tents. Chow lines were a quarter mile long. Orders for the First Army alone filled a book thicker than "Gone With the Wind." Other GIs studied French phrase books including how to say "My wife doesn't understand me" which caused a flap back home.

The Slapton Sands on the Channel coast were made into replicas of Utah and Omaha beaches, where the GIs were to land, and Gold, Sword and Juno, where the British and Canadians would. On April 28, some swift German E-boats got among the practicing fleet and 749 Americans were killed.

Instructions were incredibly detailed. Paratroopers of the 506th Battalion, 101st Airborne Division were briefed that the gun commander of their objective in St. Come-de-Mont owned a white horse, was dating a French school teacher, lived one house from his battery and walked his dog every evening at 2000 hours.

Right to the end, Churchill argued for some less risky operation such as "a dagger under the armpit" by invading Yugoslavia near Trieste and swinging through the Lubljana Gap to Vienna. Roosevelt wired him: "I would never survive even a minor setback in Normandy if it were known that substantial troops were diverted to the Balkans." Churchill was enraged at such "bullying." For his part, Marshall was concerned that Eisenhower had come down with "theateritis," undue influence by his British associates. He sent him a stern letter.

Normandy it was to be or nothing. The Channel ports of the Pas-de-Calais were too small. Normandy offered quick access to the interior and the seaports of Brittany. At Montgomery's insistence, the landing force was increased to eight divisions including three airborne and three armored brigades. Ahead of them were 56 divisions Field Marshal von Rundstedt had within 200 miles of Normandy.

* * * *

Even though German planes flew only 129 sorties over England in the six weeks prior to D-Day, it was obvious something was coming. But where?

Norway? The British created a fictitious army in Scotland. Wedding announcements of its "soldiers" were placed in local newspapers as well as scores of soccer games between its "teams." Radio traffic to the Norwegian underground asked for weather and snow conditions and the amount of alpine gear the Germans had.

Calais? Another phantom army sprang up southeast of London, this one commanded by Patton, still in the doghouse. Fake landing barges were festooned with laundry and gave out real exhaust smoke. Genuine tanks left tracks in the sod next to dummy ones. Real messages were phoned to a radio

A reconnaissance plane photographs the ground on D-Day, gliders strewn among the hedgerows of Normandy which were to reduce tank warfare to a crawl. The English Channel is in upper right corner.

transmitter at the "army's" location which broadcast the inconsequential ones back to the real Allied encampments to cement the illusion to German listeners that the fictitious "1st Army Group" really was stationed in Kent hard by the Channel invasion ports.

The Balkans? A Montgomery look-alike was dispatched to Gibraltar to give weight to planted rumors. Hitler moved three divisions south.

Keeping the real secret had security tearing their hair. A dozen copies of invasion plans blew out a window at the War Office. Frantic employees recaptured 11. The 12th turned up two hours later. A passerby had given it to a Life Guards horseman. A postal clerk in Chicago opened a package of plans an American had sent by mistake to his sister. In May, one Leonard Sidney Dawe, a physics professor who constructed crossword puzzles for the Daily Telegraph, was taken aback when visited by British counterintelligence. They wanted to know why over five days his puzzles had clues answered by Utah, Omaha, Overlord and Neptune — the code name for the landing itself — and Mulberry, the planned artificial harbors. Coincidence, said Dawe. Indeed.

Operation Taxable was designed to give German radars in the Pas-de-Calais plane-like echoes from barrage balloons and aluminum chaff. Operation Glimmer made recordings of anchor chains and other nautical noises to be broadcast off that coast. Radios of Operation Chatter were tuned to Luftwaffe frequencies to give erroneous messages in German. Meanwhile Allied planes bombed railroad hubs around the clock. Eighteen of 24 bridges over the Seine between Paris and the sea were destroyed. Back in the camps, men dressed as Germans strolled about to familiarize the troops with what the enemy looked like.

By the time Operation Fortitude, the whole panoply of deception, reached its peak, the Germans estimated there were 92 to 97 divisions in England

ready to pounce. Actually, there were 35. Of 250 agents reporting to Himmler, all were wrong about the invasion but one. Rommel, in command in Normandy, insisted the invaders be thrown back at the beach line if Germany were to prevail. Von Rundstedt planned a defense in depth, then attack. Allied planes wouldn't allow this, Rommel insisted. Hitler sided with Rommel. "If we don't throw the invaders back, we can't win a static war because of the materiel our enemies can bring in."

Then a poem by Paul Verlaine almost blew the whole thing.

Every evening the BBC broadcast cryptic messages to the underground: "The dice are on the table." "It is hot in Suez." "The Trojan War will not be held." One message had been two lines from Verlaine's "The Song of Autumn." The first — "The

Surviving American glider pilots, their D-Day work done, catch a smoke as they ferry to a transport back to England.

long sobs of the violins of autumn" — was an alert. The second — "Wounding my heart with a monotonous langour" — was an execute order. It had been used once before, compromised and abandoned. But by a momentous boo-boo it was reinstated to notify the Maquis, the French underground, that the invasion was coming within 48 hours. The Gestapo forced the code's significance from a captured Maquisard. They picked up the first line June 1, the second June 5. Von Rundstedt and Hitler were alerted. Rommel was away on leave and couldn't be reached. And nobody told Col. Gen. Friedrich Dollmann's 7th Army. In Normandy.

* * * *

Group Capt. James M. Stagg walked around with his own cloud. "There goes 6-feet-2 of Stagg and 6-feet-1 of gloom," they used to say at the RAF base where he was the weatherman. Now he was calling the shots for the biggest gamble of the war.

From June 1 on, Stagg presented his forecasts at 9:30 p.m. and 4 a.m. to Eisenhower and his staff at Southwick House near Portsmouth. The ideal window for D-Day was for a dawn tide just on the rise and a full moon. June 6 was the last chance until June 19 when there would be no moon for the paratroopers. The weather continued poor. John Lyman, a Harvard lawyer turned gunner, waited aboard an LST. "It was raining like hell, and we sat for hours. Finally, we were told: 'It isn't on. The weather's too icky-poo.'"

"When I die, they ought to hold my body for a rainy day," Eisenhower said. But at the evening meeting June 4, Stagg reported that an unexpected high had developed off Spain and was moving towards Normandy. June 6 would be clear in the morning, then cloud up. Rear Adm. Alan G. Kirk had to know in half an hour whether or not the invasion was on. If not, he would have to refuel, forcing a 48-hour postponement. "I don't see how we can do anything else," Ike said. At the 4 a.m. meeting June 5 the high was still moving.

"O.K.," said Eisenhower. "We'll go."

On June 4, the 101st was given ice cream for the first time in the nine months they had been in Britain. They were treated to a movie: "Mr. Lucky" starring Cary Grant and Laraine Day. The next day at 2030, loaded down with more than a hundred pounds of gear from small mines to Cracker-Jack clickers to signal each other, they headed for the

planes. "It was like a death march," a paratrooper recalled. "It was the first time I'd ever seen any real emotion from a limey. They had tears in their eyes." Bill Guarnere of the 101st Screaming Eagles had just received news from home. His brother had been killed at Cassino. "I swore that when I got to Normandy... they had turned a killer loose."

Sgt. Harold Williams marched down a pier to embark. An elderly woman, in tears, kept saying to the Yanks: "Thank you, lads, for helping us out."

Some British troops marching to their LST stopped to watch a cricket match. A sniper spied on a pair of distant lovers through his 'scope.

There were 5,700 ships at sea including seven battleships. One was the Nevada, raised from the mud of Pearl Harbor. There were the cruiser Augusta that carried Roosevelt to the Newfoundland meeting with Churchill and Britain's Ajax, which hounded the pocket battleship Graf Spee to its doom. At "Piccadilly Circus," a spot 13 miles southeast of the Isle of Wight, they formed into five task forces and headed for France. "Where's the officers' life raft?" asked a cavalry blueblood aboard a British transport. Aboard his LST, John Lyman's battery was given the sailors' chicken supply as a farewell dinner.

Percy Wallace, the lighthouse keeper on St. Gibans Head, watched the armada and asked his wife to kneel with him. "A lot of men are going to die tonight. We should pray for them."

* * * *

The paratroopers went in first. The U.S. 82nd and 101st — 13,000 men — were to drop inland from the westernmost beach, Utah, target of the 4th Infantry Division. The British 6th Airborne Division was to come down behind Sword beach towards Caen, to be taken the first day. (It took Montgomery a month.)

Skies were clear for the Americans until they ran into clouds over the coast. Formation broke down. Pilots speeded up to get out of there. The drop was strewn over 100 square miles. Seven men refused to jump. Eleven men of Cpl. Louis Merlano's stick landed in the sea and drowned. He heard German voices and began eating his codes. Some men didn't find their units for weeks. When Pvt. Tom Burgess landed, a French farmer kissed his hand. Guarnere collected a group and quickly took some Germans prisoner. When they weren't looking, the Germans tried to jump them. Guarnere shot them. Lynn

Left: All ashore. A Coast Guard landing craft unloads another line of GIs in the D-Day assault in Normandy. Utah Beach was moderate, but German resistance on Omaha Beach caused Gen. Omar Bradley to briefly consider abandoning the landing.

Compton, an All-American catcher at UCLA, hit a German with a grenade and blew his head off. Lt. Richard Winters led a handful of 101st men on a battery of four guns zeroed in on Utah. They killed 15, took 12 prisoners, routed a platoon of German paratroopers and spiked the cannon. Pvt. John Steele's parachute snagged the clock tower at St. Mere-Eglise, and he watched helpless from on high as the 82nd fought for the village. Maj. Lawrence Legree of the 101st was challenged by some Ger-

mans, tried to explain he was coming home from a date while struggling to pull the pin on a grenade. He threw it finally and found three dead Germans. Dummy parachutists designed to explode like machine gun fire on impact and broadcast warlike recorded voices befuddled the German defenders as they dropped all over Normandy. "The Americans knew what was happening but few of them knew where they were. The Germans knew where they were, but none of them knew what was happening," writes David Howarth in his book on D-Day.

Ultra intercepted welcome news. The German weathermen had not picked up Stagg's clearing front. Their forecast was for stormy weather. No invaders would be out on a day like that. The invasion exercise for top commanders in Normandy would go on in Rennes in Brittany, far from the beaches, as scheduled.

As dawn broke, Maj. Werner Pluskat, whose

They called the Normandy beach obstacles "Rommel's Asparagus." The German commander in Normandy was home for his wife's birthday on D-Day, but his invasion barriers were a bothersome presence.

DE GAULLE

As if there weren't enough problems on that momentous June 6, there was also Charles de Gaulle. Not in on the invasion date, he withdrew French liaison officers from the landing task force. He broadcast that the invaders' landing scrip was counterfeit. Then he demanded to be taken to Normandy in a battleship. He'll go in a landing craft "just like the rest of us," said Gen. Tom Handy, Marshall's aide.

D-Day night, de Gaulle broadcast to his people. He did mention the British but not the Americans. "No sons of Iowa farmers would fight to put up statues of de Gaulle in France," snorted Marshall. Then the Frenchman worsened the situation by announcing in his broadcast: "The battle has begun." This horrified Fortitude planners still trying to convince Hitler only *one* battle had begun. Garbo got on the air to Berlin with more disinformation of a coming second landing. The BBC put out a barrage of floral and rain-in-Spain messages to the Belgian and Pas-de-Calais undergrounds. Berlin was so impressed it put Garbo in for an Iron Cross that very day. It should have been the order of the double cross.

In the final analysis, the fate of the D-Day landing rested with the foot soldier, his gun and his courage.

battery was above Omaha Beach, scanned the horizon with his binoculars. There was nothing but ships. He called headquarters. Where were the ships headed? "Right for me!"

Gen. Hans Spiedel, Rommel's chief of staff, was alerted at headquarters in the chateau at La Roche-Guyon, well to the rear. He had just finished drinks with conspirators plotting to kill Hitler. "For the time being this is not to be considered a large operation," he decided. The chateau was the seat of the dukes of La Rochefoucauld, one of whom, Francois, was France's great epigrammist. *"C'est une grande habilete que de savoir cacher son habilete,"* he had written. The height of cleverness is to be able to conceal it. He could have been talking about the ruses of Fortitude.

Omaha was the worst. The 1st and 29th Divisions landed there. As Sgt. Roy Stevens of the 29th was boarding his landing craft, he met his brother and tried to shake hands. "No, we'll shake hands at the

crossroads in France just as we planned." Stevens never saw him again. Capt. Edmund Duckworth of the 1st was killed as he stepped ashore. He had married an English girl five days before. A landing barge began to founder in four-foot waves. To lighten ship, gear was tossed overboard. With it went Pvt. Chuck Vella's $1,200 winnings from a crap game and Sgt. Charles Frederick's false teeth. A company of Rangers lost half its 70 men before it could reach the seawall 300 yards from the water on Omaha. By nightfall, 12 remained. Twenty-seven of 32 floating tanks, a special design for the landing, went down, most with their crews. A medic stitched the gashed thigh of a GI with safety pins. A Company of the 116th Regiment landed with 197 men and suffered 96 percent casualties. "Within 20 minutes, A Company had become a forlorn little rescue party bent upon survival," the official history recorded. Twenty of the dead were from the small town of Bedford, Virginia. Capt. Carroll Smith of the 29th saw the body of his friend, Capt. Sherman Burroughs, rolling in the surf, shot through the head. At least he won't be having any more migraines, Smith thought.

Bulldozers were meant to clear a path up and over the bluff in back of Omaha. Only three of 16 made it

With a toehold on the Normandy beaches, American men and vehicles began the first steps inland.

ashore. Just before a path through the anti-tank barriers was to be blown, a tank ran over the detonating wire. The first wave was 3,000 men. More kept coming. Ernest Hemingway, a correspondent on Omaha, wrote: "The first, second, third, fourth and fifth waves lay where they had fallen, looking like so many heavily laden bundles on the flat pebbly stretch between the sea and the first cover."

"Two kinds of people are staying on this beach," hollered Col. George Taylor, "the dead and those who are going to die. Now let's get the hell out of here!" Col. Charles Canham put it bluntly to his men: "They're murdering us here. Let's move inland and get murdered."

Gradually they did so. Bradley had weighed ordering the men taken off. Now he reconsidered.

Lt. P.K. Smith of the 1st Division proudly had held his breakfast down as his landing craft rolled towards the beach. Ducking shrapnel, he lowered his head towards the bilge with its diesel fumes and hit the beach seasick. As the Big Red One fought to the bluffs, Smith ordered in fire from the big guns of the battleships, as much out of curiosity to see a 16-inch shell explode as to smite the enemy. Omaha now had room for a whim.

On Utah, Maj. Gen. Theodore Roosevelt, a president's son, second in command of the 4th and at 57 the oldest man on the beach, strode with his cane and seven-shot automatic with the aplomb of a beachfront buyer instead of invader. He rallied his men up the dunes and won a Medal of Honor for it. He got it the day he died of a heart attack.

Nazi troopers in Russia trudge along a railroad beneath a prophetic sign: "All Will Have Its End."

ARMY GROUP CENTER

In return for the second front, Stalin as promised attacked June 22 with 166 divisions on a 450-mile front in White Russia, now Belarus. It was a reversal of Barbarossa three years before. On July 3, Minsk fell. Germany's Army Group Center of 350,000 men simply evaporated. The OKW Journal called it a "greater catastrophe than Stalingrad." The Red Army under Zhukov marched 400 miles to the gates of Warsaw. Thinking deliverance was at hand, the Polish underground revolted. Whether the Soviets were too exhausted to fight into the city or wanted non-communists eradicated by the Germans remains disputed.

In the Ukraine and Crimea, the offensive recaptured Sevastapol, which had withstood a German siege for 250 days in 1941-42, in five days plus 60,000 prisoners. The Russians swept 400 miles through Romania in 18 days, taking the Ploesti oil fields. In all, the Wehrmacht suffered 672,000 casualties in the battles. Romania and Finland, both reluctant German allies, (the Finns had declared war on Russia, but not on the United States and Britain) switched sides and declared war on Hitler. In November, the Germans began a 600-mile retreat from Greece. Another ebb tide.

Lt. Marty Lederhandler, an Associated Press photographer then with the Signal Corps, attached some film to a carrier pigeon. The bird flew east instead of to London. The photos eventually appeared in a German newspaper.

To the east, the British paratroopers in furious hand-to-hand fighting silenced a major German battery just 15 minutes before it was to be bombarded by warships. "Battery taken as ordered, Sir. Guns destroyed," reported Lt. Mike Dowling. Then he fell dead. On Juno, a Canadian tank with hatches closed was crushing wounded as it ran down the beach until an officer blew off a tread with a hand grenade. A sailor looking for a souvenir helmet tracked a Canadian herding six German POWs behind a sand dune. He found them dead, their throats slashed. Four Germans met some British at the water's edge with packed suitcases ready for prison camp in England. At Pointe du Hoc, 220

Rangers heroically scaled a sheer cliff with ladders borrowed from the London Fire Department to attack a vital battery. The guns hadn't been emplaced yet.

Ferocity on the beaches quickly escalated. Soldiers of the 12th Panzer Division, made up of young zealots of the Hitler Youth program, shot a group of more than 60 prisoners in cold blood. A GI ordered one of his prisoners to run, then shot him and directed a tank to run over the body. A paratrooper killed some German prisoners who tried to overpower him. "No remorse. No pity. It was easy as stepping on a bug."

At sea, destroyers moved in so close their bottoms scraped as they fired point blank. But bombers which meant to soften up the beachheads missed in all the smoke and dust and dropped their loads harmlessly inland. From England, two turned German spies, code-named Brutus and Garbo, radioed

Crippled German tanks in a Normandy farm field attest to Allied air supremacy and the power of massed artillery.

Germany of the imminent departure of troops from Dover to the Pas-de-Calais. Smoke screens were laid in the Channel to persuade von Rundstedt another landing was heading his way.

He had ordered two panzer divisions to move up, but sent one to Deauville on the Pas-de-Calais. Col. Gen. Alfred Jodl, chief of staff of the OKW, countermanded the order. Von Rundstedt thereupon spent the morning pruning roses at his headquarters outside Paris.

Knowing Hitler was another night owl, Jodl did not want to wake him with news of the landing. Hitler awoke at 10 a.m. at his alpine lair at Berchtesgaden, cordially greeted everyone and said the Allies were also going to land on the Channel. Then he sat down for a vegetarian lunch with the new prime minister of Hungary. He told von Rundstedt he could move the two panzers to Normandy but no more. Then he lay down for a nap.

Von Rundstedt was livid. "His anger made his speech unintelligible," his aides said. But the man the general called "that Bohemian corporal" had the last word.

Word reached Rommel at 10:15 a.m. at his home in Bavaria where he had gone to celebrate his wife's birthday. "I was right all along, all along," he said as his aide, Capt. Hellmuth Lang, sped him back to La Roche-Guyon. Earlier he had told Lang: "The first 24 hours of the invasion will be decisive ... for the Allies as well as Germany it will be the longest day." And he had made a very late start.

The one panzer attack of the day was launched by Gen. Erich Marcks. He told Col. Hermann von Oppeln-Bronikowski: "If you don't succeed in throwing the British into the sea, we've lost the war." The drive petered out after the Germans lost 70 of their 124 tanks. Bronikowski watched a drunken soldier and two Wehrmacht women stagger up the road and thought to himself: "The war is lost."

By nightfall the Allies had 55,000 men ashore. Omaha's beachhead was six miles wide and two deep. On Utah, too, the GIs had moved inland. They had suffered only 197 casualties. The Allies had flown 10,585 missions to less than 319 for the Luftwaffe, which had only 119 operational fighters. With complete air supremacy, supplies poured ashore. A scout from Utah probed inland. He met a paratrooper from the 101st, Sgt. Thomas Bruff.

"Where's the war?" the scout asked. "Keep going, buddy," Bruff answered, "You'll find it."

19

"COBRA"

1944

The phone rang in von Rundstedt's headquarters. It was Hitler's perplexed bootlicker, Field Marshal Wilhelm Keitel, OKW chief of staff. "What shall we do?" A proper question.

By that July 1 day, the Allies had 1 million men ashore, 172,000 vehicles, complete air supremacy.

Above: *Hitler ordered the Cherbourg garrison to fight to the last man. They surrendered instead. Troops in other French ports in Brittany were bottled up and lost to the Nazis because of Hitler's refusal to allow withdrawal.*

Left: Out of the doghouse, Patton, left, arrives in Normandy to meet with U.S. land commander, Omar Bradley, center, and overall ground leader, Britain's Bernard Montgomery, a man neither American would come to love.

Within weeks, German casualties were to total 117,000 men with only 20,000 replacements. Three of the four divisions in the LXXXIV Corps would be down to only 2,500 riflemen in toto. Communications were so disrupted the 276th Infantry Division took 19 days to get from Nice to Normandy. The 275th Division came in on bikes.

What to do? "End the war, stupid," von Rundstedt answered. "What else can you do?" The next day, July 2, he resigned. But the Allies were still bottled up in Normandy.

"We couldn't understand why they didn't break through," said Cpl. Adolf Hohenstein of the 276th.

One reason was the American style of warfare. "Never send an infantryman to do a job the artillery can do for him," said Lt. Gen. William H. Simpson. "At the smallest resistance to the enemy, he stops and retires and a new artillery bombardment takes place," said a panzer commander. "In defense, the enemy is a hard fighter only so long as he has good

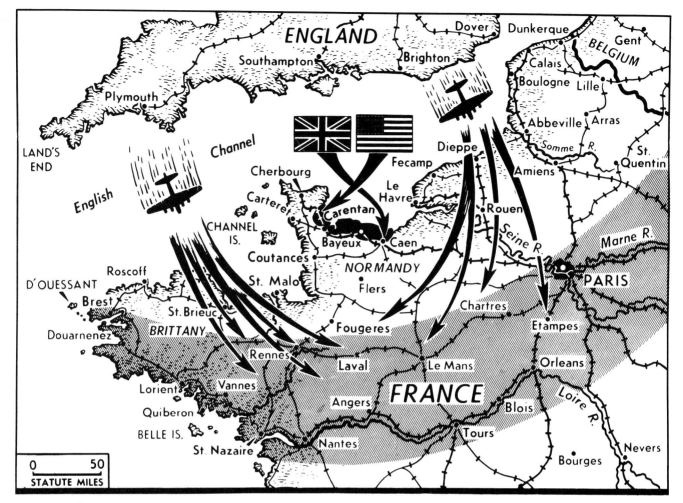

Map indicating the progress of the Allies four days after the D-Day landing. Blackened coast shows land held by the Allies. Shaded area covers range of targets for supporting bomber attacks.

support from artillery." To Americans, shells were cheaper than lives. This did not make for blitzkrieg, but it worked, slowly.

"I don't have to tell you who won the war. Our artillery did." That was George Patton's comment. He was back in good graces in command of the Third Army, an armored spearhead ready to roll.

Another holdup was the *bocage* of Normandy, ancient overgrown hedgerows that were natural tank barriers. They weren't solved until a Tennessee GI named "Hillbilly" Roberts asked why they didn't put earth-moving prongs on the tanks. Lt. Gen. J. Lawton "Lightning Joe" Collins' men then closed off the Cotentin peninsula and captured the port of Cherbourg June 27. "Stop!" cried a GI as he burst into a Cherbourg bunker where German officers were sitting down to a ham dinner. "I'll take that."

THE Vs

On June 13, 1944, Hitler launched the first of the "secret weapons" he thought would win the war. This was the V-1, a subsonic flying bomb powered by a ram jet engine. One of a first salvo of 10 hit London, killing six civilians. They were to kill 6,200 people and damage 750,000 buildings. But air defenses improved, and on August 28, 90 of 98 were shot down. On September 1, most of their launch sites were captured.

But a week later the first V-2 was fired. This was a true rocket, the ancestor of today's ballistic missiles. Five hundred were launched over the next seven months killing another 2,700 Britons.

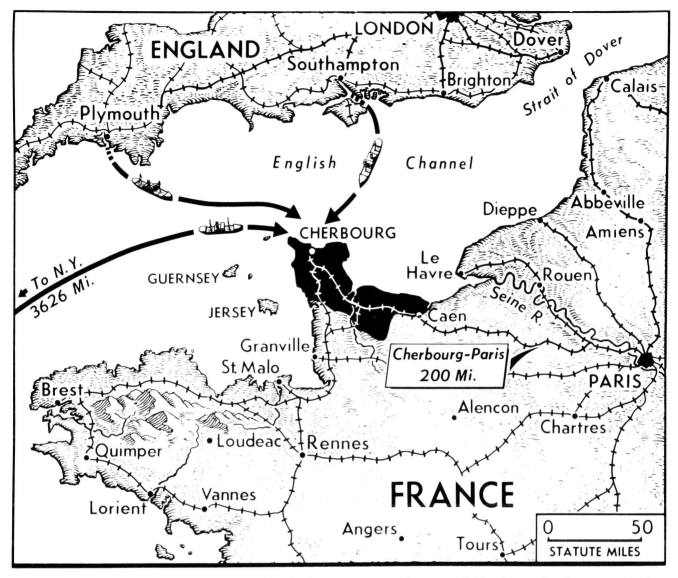

Once Cherbourg was opened to Allied shipping, supplies could be brought from ports in England and the U.S.

The Americans also took the garrison Hitler thought would hold out three months. The first ship came in two days later, but the port had been so wrecked by the Germans, it wasn't operational until September.

After finally capturing Caen, Montgomery on July 18 launched Operation Goodwood to break into the open. Some 8,000 tanks and vehicles were assembled, but panzer commander Sepp Dietrich said he knew they were coming just by putting his ear to the ground. Despite an immense preliminary air barrage, the Germans stopped Goodwood, named for Britain's second most prestigious racehorse meeting, cold. Montgomery found himself swallow-

ing his overeager claims of success. Eisenhower was so furious aides feared he'd have a heart attack.

Said the Supreme Commander of Monty: "He was slow. He never did anything as quickly as anyone else did. And he was always bellyaching....Somebody just ought to smack him down."

But Montgomery's loss of 400 tanks was made up in 36 hours. The German loss of 109 was not. They had only 17 in reserve.

Sometimes the British astounded the Americans in other ways. John Lyman remembers one tank regiment in Normandy "stood to" every afternoon at 5 o'clock in front of their machines which were started to make sure they worked. "Well, the Ger-

The hedgerows of Normandy, the **bocage**, *were natural fortifications for the Germans, endless hurdles for the invaders.*

mans found out about this and shelled them every day at 5 o'clock. But do you think the British would change the routine? Certainly not."

On July 25, Lt. Gen. Fritz Bayerlein's once-crack Panzer Lehr Division was reduced to only a fraction of the 182 tanks he had when rushed to Normandy in June. That morning, Operation Cobra, the long-expected breakout, began. The bombers came first, carpet bombing with crater-free lanes left for tanks. The Germans fired American signal flares into the target zone to mislead the aircraft. That and overly precise aiming caused some bombs to fall short. Numerous Americans, including Lt. Gen. Lesley McNair, one of Marshall's key aides, were killed.

"The planes kept coming over as if on a conveyor belt," said Bayerlein. "Nothing was visible but dust and smoke ... Front lines looked like the face of the moon, and at least 70 percent of my troops were out of action, and the roads were practically impassable. The shock effect was indescribable. Several of my men went mad."

Against air supremacy "all the courage didn't help," said Rommel. "There is no longer anything we can do. Victory in a major battle on the continent seems to me a matter of grave doubt." Rommel was considering privately negotiating with the Allies when a strafing attack crashed his limousine, gravely injuring him. The Desert Fox was out of the war.

After the 1,800 bombers were through, Bradley

Allied tanks were stymied by the thick hedgerows of Normandy until a GI devised these plow-like prongs. These were fashioned from German beach tank traps.

unleashed 15 divisions and 750 tanks centered on what was left of St. Lo. Then came Patton.

Out in the clear, his tanks turned right into Brittany, home of the major U-boat bases. Third Army captured the old Breton capital of Rennes August 4. Then Bradley changed the original Cobra plan and sent Patton east through LeMans and Orleans and to the south of Paris. Bradley was right, but he should have freed Patton sooner.

Instead of retreating while he could — "He's worth 40 divisions to us," said Brooke of the Fuhrer's battlefield blunders — Hitler ordered a desperation attack to cut off the Third Army by taking Avranches on the coast between Normandy and Brittany. The attack came August 6 and was finally

stopped by a heroic stand of a battalion of the 30th Division. Von Rundstedt's successor, Field Marshal Gunther Hans von Kluge, ordered Bayerlein to hold to the last man. "Out in front everyone is holding out. Everyone," Bayerlein replied in white heat. "Not a single man is leaving his post. They are lying silently in their foxholes, for they are dead. You understand? Dead ... The Panzer Lehr Division is annihilated!"

Bradley then tripped up again, ordering Patton not to close the trap on the whole German army in Normandy at Falaise. He feared it would interfere with Polish and Canadian troops closing the pocket from the north. Nevertheless, while 50,000 Germans escaped with little more than their clothing, 240,000 more were caught in a killing ground. British Typhoon fighter-bombers raked the pocket. The stench of dead men and horses was so strong spotter planes flew higher to escape it. Ten divisions surrendered, as big a haul as Stalingrad. For the Allies, 36,976 had died. The 90th Division alone had lost 150 percent of its original officer strength and 100 percent of its original enlisted men. But now Normandy was behind them.

* * * *

The French 2nd Armored Division of Brig. Gen. Jacques Leclerc liberated Paris August 25 to a tumultuous reception while the Maquis fought in the streets against a few remaining Germans. Capt. Raymond Sarniguet of the Fire Brigade climbed the 1,750 steps of the Eiffel Tower to fly the French tricolor he had taken down in 1940. De Gaulle defied snipers to march down the Champs Elysees and into Notre Dame. A German fled from the Hotel Ritz like a tourist, his arms filled with perfume and soap. A Parisian mob stomped him to death. Ernest Hemingway bought martinis all around for 73 Maquisards with him and settled for a bottle of Piper Heidsieck champagne for himself at the Hotel Scribe. Maj. Gen. Norman Cota, one of the heroes of Omaha Beach, paraded his 28th Infantry Division into town at French request and then right back out again, back to the war.

Patton, too, had kept on going, bypassing Paris and motoring unopposed to Metz and Nancy. Up until October the Allies "could have broken through at any point with ease...crossed the Rhine and thrust deep into Germany almost unhindered," said Gen. Siegrfried Westphal, a staff officer. Instead, in late September, the Third Army ran out of gas, literally. Eisenhower had ordered Patton to halt and gave priority to Montgomery who was slicing through the German 15th Army which had been foolishly based in the Pas-de-Calais throughout.

Montgomery was to get five tons of supplies to every two for Patton in order to capture the V-2 sites plus Antwerp, which was to be the main Allied port. As early as June 8, the Germans had recovered plans from the body of an American officer which established conclusively that Normandy was the only invasion target. But Hitler insisted the 15th Army stay in place along the Channel to repulse an invasion that never came.

Meanwhile, Americans and French troops of Op-

"VALKYRIE"

Col. Claus von Stauffenberg, an aristocratic war hero who had lost an arm, eye and most of his remaining hand in Africa, attended a staff meeting at Hitler's Wolf's Lair July 20, 1944. He excused himself at one point, leaving behind a tan leather briefcase next to Hitler's chair. Someone moved it to the other side of a stout oak table leg from the Fuhrer. It saved his life when two pounds of plastic exploded.

The bomb killed four but only left Hitler temporarily deafened, his pants shredded and his behind, he told Mussolini who visited later that day, looking like "the backside of a baboon."

The plotters of Operation Valkyrie, originally a standby mobilization plan should slave labor in Germany ever revolt, hesitated and bungled, key troops remained loyal and the plot was crushed by nightfall. Rommel, who knew of it, was forced to commit suicide. Von Kluge, implicated, did the same. In all, 11,448 suspected plotters were killed, many photographed as they strangled from piano wire hung on meat hooks to delight Hitler's entourage. The reign of terror took the life as well of Adm. Canaris, head of the Abwehr and possible conduit to the Allies.

eration Dragoon had landed on August 15 in southern France unopposed — except by strenuous objections from the British who still wanted to invade the Balkans. In top-gear road marches they moved up to become Patton's right flank. Dragoon soon proved itself, as Marseilles transshipped half of all the supplies for the Third Army.

Stopping him in favor of Montgomery was, said Patton, "the most momentous error of the war" and many agree. His daily allotment of fuel over the badly-overburdened, 24-hour 40-miles-an-hour-or-

At de Gaulle's request, U.S. troops of the 28th Division marched down the Champs Elysee where Nazis had paraded four years earlier. Then they marched out of town to resume the war.

Lucky German survivors of the Falaise pocket. The stench of thousands of dead was so strong artillery spotters flew at higher altitudes.

get-off-the-road trucks of the Red Ball Express was 32,000 gallons instead of 400,000. He ordered his tankers to drive until empty, "then get out and walk." Monty had lobbied Ike for permission to make "a knife thrust into Germany and the Lowlands." "More like a butter knife thrust," Patton told Bradley as Montgomery was inexcusably slow in clearing the Scheldt estuary to open Antwerp, letting yet more Germans escape.

Eisenhower was made direct commander of the battle September 1, much to Montgomery's displeasure. To calm him down, he was made a field marshal — making him senior to Ike in rank although subordinate. Eisenhower's plan was for parallel offensives by Americans through the Siegfried Line into the Ruhr with Montgomery attacking along the north German plains. He wanted options. On September 10, Montgomery asked Eisenhower to visit him (the Briton made it a point of never returning the courtesy, "too busy," he'd say) and berated his plans as "balls, rubbish, balls!" Restraining himself, Ike put his hand on the new field marshal's knee: "Steady, Monty. You can't talk to me like that. I'm your boss."

"I'm sorry, Ike," he mumbled, then outlined *his* plans: a parachute drop across the Rhine at a Dutch town called Arnhem.

Allied forces in Italy preparing for the invasion of Southern France.

20

"MARKET-GARDEN"

1944

The boldness of Montgomery's plan dumbfounded Omar Bradley, no admirer.

"Had the pious, teetotalling Montgomery wobbled into SHAEF with a hangover, I could not have been more astonished than I was by the daring adventure he proposed."

Both Bradley and Patton had been brought to the point of resigning over Eisenhower's seeming par-

A bold gamble to sieze the Rhine bridge at Arnhem in the Netherlands with a combination glider paratroop drop fell short as German resistance in the flooded lowlands held up the Allied relief column. U.S. gliders shown here landed at Nijmegen.

Its engine cut out, a German "buzz" bomb heads earthward. During the summer of 1944, Germany bombarded London with V-1 flying bombs and V-2 rocket missiles. Allied advances in France, Belgium and Holland deprived Germany of its launching sites for these weapons.

tiality to Montgomery, including temporarily assigning him the American 1st Army. But they agreed Operation Market-Garden might be a decisive stroke. It involved drops by the 82nd and 101st to take Eindhoven and Njimegen in southern Holland and hold a single two-lane highway through the swamped flatlands for Lt. Gen. Brian Horrock's XXX Corps to reach the British 1st Airborne dropped near Arnhem and its key river bridge over the Rhine. Horrocks' Britons would have to travel 64 miles and cross five rivers and canals. Lt. Gen. Frederick Browning, commander of the British I Airborne

Corps, told Montgomery he could hold out four days. "But I think, sir, we may be going a bridge too far."

Market-Garden was only a week in planning. On September 17, the paratroopers came down like blossoms from a tree. Browning, aristocratic husband of novelist Daphne du Maurier, dashed a few feet into Germany. "I wanted to be the first British officer to pee there." (Churchill and Patton did the same when they crossed the Rhine later in the war.) One Red Devil stopped for tea at an inn. Another paused in a hayloft in the welcoming arms of a

Dutch girl. Both Ultra and the Dutch underground cautioned that two panzer divisions were in the area, but the British dismissed the warning. When Maj. Brian Urquhart of paratroop intelligence noted tanks under trees in photo reconnaissance, it was suggested he was tired and should take some time off.

Many tides had turned against the Germans, but they still had 3.4 million men under arms. U-boat crews and the Luftwaffe had been given rifles and joined the infantry. Twenty-five militia divisions had been called up and 18 new divisions created from wounded, clerks and city policemen fresh from their beats. One unit, the "stomach division," was comprised only of men with intestinal problems who were fed special bread. Top-flight divisions still existed in the Wehrmacht, and two of them, both panzers, were indeed under the trees at Arnhem, right where the 1st Airborne was headed.

Col. John Frost had jumped with 10,005 other Red Devils but arranged for his dinner jacket and golf clubs to be flown in later. However, the men had landed six long miles from the bridge. Frost and his men captured the north end of the bridge, but German tanks fought off efforts by Capt. Eric Mackay to take the southern end. They held out five days in one of the war's illustrious stands. Notable was Maj. Digby Tatham-Warter who strolled about the battlefield with an umbrella. He needed it for identification, he explained. "I was always forget-

ting the password." Mackay was finally captured, telling an astonished German officer: "It is all over for Germany, and I am quite prepared to take your surrender." He escaped, was recaptured, escaped again and finally made it back to the Allied lines, one of only 2,163 Red Devils to do so.

The American troopers had been delayed by delirious Hollanders waving the national orange, then fierce German resistance.

Maj. Julian Cook led 254 men of the 82nd across the 400-yard-wide Waal River into a murderous barrage from Germany's best weapons, the 88s and Spandau machine guns. Paddling rubber rafts with their helmets and rifle butts, the men gained the far shore having lost 134 killed. They were only 11 miles from Arnhem.

But German guns picked off Horrocks's tanks as they came single file up the highway. They had to wait for the airborne to clear the way.

"I am proud to meet the commander of the greatest division in the world today," said Gen. Miles Dempsey of Britain's 2nd Army, shaking hands with Brig. Gen. James Gavin of the 82nd.

But Col. Reuben Tucker of the 82nd fumed that the British tanks didn't just keep coming. "That's what George Patton would have done ... As usual, they stopped for tea." They never made it.

After nine heroic days, the Red Devils, minced into ever smaller pieces, were finally overrun. It *had* been one bridge too far.

21

"HERBSTNEBEL"

1944-45

One last time it was the deep, silent forest of the Ardennes. It was there, in the spring, when France began to fall. It was there, four years later as the coldest winter in Europe in 54 years began, there in the snow, there that the American Army came of age.

It had been a long maturity for this citizen army, and a hard one. Marshall paid tribute to the GIs he was so instrumental in shaping, millions of men "thousands of miles from home in places they had hardly heard of. There was none of the tremendous spirit that comes from defending your own home." Of the British soldier, he said: "Very stolid ... ac-

Above: *The Bulge was fought in the coldest winter in Europe in decades. But U.S. tanks like these kept moving, snow or no.*

Left: *On the defensive everywhere in 1944, Germany still had fanatic fighters such as this trooper in Belgium.*

cepted losses they had to." The Russian: "Not an intelligent soldier ... but he had the courage to go ahead, though he didn't understand why, if (leadership) was any way decent." And the German? "Natural fighters ... discipline unbending."

Germany had lost upwards of 3 million men thus far. Its cities were bombed by day and by night. Life had been reduced to essentials. All theaters were closed. All men 16 to 60 were drafted; slave labor would keep the factories running. The staff of the Berlin Opera was put to work in an electrical plant. Only in the countryside was food abundant. Yet the nation fought on. Conquest was no longer the issue. Survival was. If anything, the German soldier fought even harder.

Why? By any rational yardstick the war had long been lost. At Stalingrad. At Kursk. In Normandy. Underneath the rolling North Atlantic. Above, long ago, in the summer skies over England. Why prolong the inevitable? There were probably as many

HUERTGEN

To cover the southern flank of a drive into Germany for Cologne, on September 14 parts of the U.S. 1st Army attacked into the Hansel and Gretel-like forest near Huertgen southeast of Aachen. "It was," said Gen. Gavin, "an impenetrable mass, a vast undulating, blackish-green ocean stretching as far as the eye can see." The Germans "could not understand the reason for a strong American attack — the fighting in the wooded area denied the advantages afforded them by their air and armored forces."

For nine weeks the battle raged, five American divisions attacking in turn. The 28th "Bloody Bucket" Division suffered 6,000 casualties, one for every yard gained. Allied planes were powerless to help the battle, invisible in the trees below. In all, 24,000 Americans were killed in what Gavin called "one of the most ill-advised battles that our army ever fought."

"OCTAGON"

Scene: Quebec's second Summit, September 1944.

Plot: Revival of previous. Churchill still wants to invade Dalmatia. Gen. Alexander: "Winston's a gambler." Largest British army, 16 divisions, is already in Italy. Roosevelt and Marshall: No Balkans. Outcome: Allies will fight anonymously as before — except for all Japanese-American 442nd Regiment, the most decorated U.S. unit of war, ultimately transferred to France — up Italy to take defensive line south of Bologna. They do and spend the winter.

answers as there were survivors who still had blood to shed. Survival, certainly, for themselves, for their loved ones, for their Fatherland. Fear, probably, fear of the retribution, particularly from the Russians, who drew ever closer. Did they still hear the siren call of Adolf Hitler? If so, would they have listened had they seen the tanks endlessly roll off Chrysler assembly lines, the bombers from Willow Run? For whatever reason, the Germans stood, fought and died.

"On a man-for-man basis, the German ground soldier consistently inflicted casualties at about a 50 percent higher rate than they incurred from opposing British and American forces under all circumstances," a postwar study concluded. The GI required 30 pounds of supplies a day, the Tommy 20. At the end of the war, the German got by with only four.

The GI was often a stranger in his own unit as replacements filled in for the fallen. One foot soldier counted 53 different lieutenants in his platoon from D-Day to V-E Day.

The GI's army was top heavy with brass: 7 percent were officers compared to 2.86 in the

Wehrmacht where the emphasis was on the leadership of veteran non-coms. And yet the GIs fought.

"A thousand times one asked oneself why," wrote Eric Sevareid of his experiences in Italy. "They understood the war's meaning no more than any others — which is to say hardly at all. Their country, their families were not in any mortal danger, and yet they plodded on...They did not hate the Germans ... They did not hate the concept of Fascism because they did not understand it. But they struggled on, climbing the hills, wading the rivers until they dropped and (died) in ignorant glory."

"Some of the fellows wanted to surrender, but we'd heard the Germans were shooting prisoners," said Charles MacGillvary who was fighting in France New Year's Day 1945. "So there really wasn't much choice but to try and get out of there." His Medal of Honor citation was more explicit. He knocked out six machine gun nests, losing an arm in the process.

How this mixed bag of Americans — draftees and volunteers, city boys and farmers — evolved into a fighting force was as varied as the millions of men involved. Rolland Webber, an airman who was shot down and imprisoned, had thought about it. "As an engineer, I tried to look at fate as a machine and find the combination of factors that made it favor some and not others. You know, character, education, ethics, everything. I never found it."

The Army found that 10 to 20 percent of riflemen suffered some kind of mental disorder in the first week of combat. "Men will break down in direct relation to the intensity of their exposure.... Most

Ike bet Montgomery five pounds the war would be over by Christmas 1944. Then Germans like these struck with unsuspected strength into the Ardennes in what became the Battle of the Bulge.

men were ineffective after 180 days or even 140.... A man reached his peak of effectiveness in the first 90 days of combat. After that, his efficiency begins to fall off." And still the Americans fought.

"I didn't have anything personal against the Krauts," said one GI after the Battle of the Bulge. "But I learned something. Now I want to kill every goddamn Kraut in the world. You know why? To save my own ass."

* * * *

And still the Germans fought: Von Rundstedt, recalled to action, because of duty, as natural to a Prussian as a ramrod spine: Field Marshal Walther Model, who would shoot himself finally, because he

was a Nazi. Von Rundstedt was titular head of Herbstnebel — Autumn Mist — but Model was in fact.

Hitler reflected the gathering ruin of his Third Reich. He had aged noticeably. His hands twitched uncontrollably. His was the desperation of the hole-card gambler. He remained convinced that his secret weapons would bring the Allies to their senses, to join him in a crusade against a common foe, the Soviet Union. Yet the daily demolition of Germany's cities, on a far greater scale than the V weapons inflicted on England, hadn't brought his people to their senses. For reasons beyond analysis, the German people remained willing to follow their Fuhrer

to their collective dooms. (This ductility to a seductive call to arms would haunt the postwar world. Would a Germany rearmed do it again?)

His leg still trembling from the assassination attempt, Hitler stunned the OKW September 16 by announcing: "I am taking the offensive." Operation Watch on the Rhine, later Autumn Mist, would split the British and American armies through the Ardennes, roll on to Antwerp at which time the Allies would have to negotiate — for reasons clear only to Hitler.

"If we reach the Meuse, we should get down on our knees and thank God," said von Rundstedt. Privately. "This damn thing doesn't have a leg to stand on," said Model. Privately.

Von Rundstedt proposed a "small solution," to swing through the Ardennes in an encircling move to trap the American 9th Army at Aachen.

The German army, mightier than the one that struck France, was assembled with great stealth. Radios were verboten, thus preventing Ultra intercepts. Only telephones were to be used. Planes flew back and forth over the Siegfried Line to cloak the noise of troop movements. There were 2,567 tanks and assault guns, 10 panzer divisions, 2,295 planes. But the tanks were only issued one-and-a-half times the standard fuel ration. Model, from his experience in Russia, wanted five times as much. The Luftwaffe pilots were young and inexperienced in spite of 65 jets in the armada. "It was Stalingrad all over again," scoffed von Rundstedt.

But the 250,000 white-clad troops were now fighting for the Fatherland. "Life is not everything," one soldier wrote his sister. "It is enough to know that we attack and will throw the enemy from our homeland. It is a holy task."

Hitler held a final meeting December 12. The war room was guarded by SS troops with machine pistols. Maj. Gen. Hans Waldenburg was afraid even to reach into his pocket for a handkerchief.

The soldiers were ordered to cook only with charcoal to avoid giveaway smoke. Von Rundstedt gave a last instruction: "We gamble everything."

The 82nd Airborne was in reserve planning for Christmas when the paratroopers were called to stem the Germans in the Bulge. Only three Allied divisions were left back in Britain.

German tanks ran out of gas, literally, in the Bulge, but U.S. tanks of the 82nd Airborne were kept fueled by the nonstop, don't-ever-drive-under-40-mph trucks of the Red Ball Express.

Ironically, Bradley had said on December 7: "If the other fellow would only hit us now." The Allies had 65 divisions on a 500-mile front: Montgomery in the north with William Simpson's 9th Army, Courtney Hodges's 1st Army in the middle, Patton in Alsace about to attack the Saar Basin, Germany's coal bin, and Jacob Devers' 7th Army and the French 1st below that. But reserves were thin. The 82nd and 101st were getting a well deserved rest at Mourmelon, an army camp since Caesar's day near Rheims. There was going to be a football game on Christmas. The only other reserves were an untried airborne division in England plus another of infantry and one armored. The weak point was the

Ardennes, a 60-mile-front running from Luxembourg City to Losheim in the north manned by only four infantry divisions and one armored. But it was so eerily quiet it was called "The Ghost Front."

* * * *

As Sgt. Donald Brownlow observed to his jeep driver: "You could hide an army in these goddamned woods and no bastard would ever know it." What with the snow and daily fog it was "like being in a glass of milk," said one GI.

The 99th Division had just moved into the line near the German-Belgian border at Butgenbach. It had yet to fire a shot in anger. Capt. Henry Reath, a gunner, drove to Losheim, a summer resort village just into Germany, to check out his forward observer. To his surprise, the observer was ensconced in someone's summer chalet, checking things out from an armchair facing the view from a second-floor picture window. Some war. The only sound of battle Lt. Brad Cochran of the 370th Artillery heard was the occasional V-1 buzzing overhead en route to London.

To the immediate right of the 99th was the 106th Division, the Golden Lions, also green as lettuce, its 16,000 men in line for hardly a week. Seven thousand men were replacements taken from specialized training programs back in the States that, with the war almost over, were no longer needed. Things were so quiet German soldiers used to sneak through the lines to visit relatives.

Monty had gone home for Christmas to be with his son. His intelligence chief, Brig. E.T. Williams, assured him: "The enemy is in a bad way.... His situation is such that he cannot stage a major operation." His counterpart with the 1st Army, Col. B.A. Dickson, wasn't so sure. "The enemy is capable of a concentrated attack ... at a selected focal point at a time of his own choosing." If so, said Tooey Spaatz, head of the U.S. Strategic Air Command, on December 15, "Now is the time. I don't think we'll be able to put a plane in the air for three days." Actually, it was nine.

Eisenhower had bet Montgomery five pounds the war would be over by Christmas. Monty tried to collect early. "I still have nine days left," said Ike. He spent the 15th at the wedding of his aide, Mickey

Try as they might, and this German paid the ultimate price, the Nazis could not break the defensive ring around besieged Bastogne.

Left: *In the Bulge, where four years before Germany's blitzkreig had doomed the French, Nazi soldiers began surrendering.*

Above: *A lone GI walks down a lane in Belgium where a group of Germans made their last stand in the snow of the Bulge.*

In the Battle of the Bulge, the American army came of age. These Germans paid the price.

McKeogh, to a WAC sergeant. Then he, Bradley and two other generals sat down with a bottle of scotch to play five rubbers of bridge.

At 5:30 a.m. the next day Lt. Lyle Bouck of the 99th remembered: "The whole horizon erupted." Ghostly Germans draped in white came out of the woods along with 60-ton tanks, the scene made more otherworldly by searchlights fingering through the fog. Fourteen-inch shells from railroad guns shattered the stillness. Five German divisions

hit the 28th Division on its 30-mile front along the River Our and penetrated six miles. Maj. Gen. Leonard Gerow of V Corps reported the offensive was "something big." At first Eisenhower wasn't too sure. Then he ordered two armored divisions be moved to Montgomery. Bradley protested. "Tell him Ike is running this damned war!" Eisenhower roared.

The confusion was compounded by Operation Greif (Griffin). English-speaking Germans dressed as Americans with American vehicles and led by Otto Skorzeny, Hitler's favorite commando who had rescued Mussolini by glider from his arrest by the Italians, infiltrated the lines and began misdirecting traffic and getting on the radio. Pop lore became the password. Brig. Gen. Bruce Clarke of the 7th Armored was jailed briefly by MPs because he insisted the Chicago Cubs were in the American League. Bradley was temporarily suspect because he insisted Chicago wasn't the capital of Illinois. Reath called Maj. Robert Ronnie at corps for a "corps barrage," the ultimate in massed artillery, to hammer 30 tanks he had spotted hiding in the trees. Ronnie, who knew him stateside, thought he recognized Reath's voice. To make sure, he said "Who's Robin?" "Robin's my daughter," Reath replied, "and fire away!" The tanks were destroyed. James Parker Cushman and his sergeant were stopped in their jeep by two seeming Americans in theirs. As one got out, Cushman noticed German field gray pants under a U.S.-issue coat. A "potato masher" grenade followed. Cushman and the sergeant drew sidearms and killed both Germans.

Herbstnebel not only had to penetrate the forest. It was also cutting against the grain of the few roads which mostly ran northeast-southwest. The key points were small road intersections, such as Bastogne, a village of 4,500 from which seven roads spoked, and St. Vith.

Cut off for three days after the initial attack, 7,000 men of the 106th surrendered, other than Bataan the largest American capitulation of the war. But behind them a combat team of the 7th Armored Division under Brig. Gen. R.W. Hasbrouck held on for five days at St. Vith. To block the road they set gasoline drums on fire.

A German pounded on the door of Capt. Dudley Britton's command post: "Cumzieout!"

"Cumzieout, hell!" Britton yelled. "What've you got out there I want? Cumzie in, Mac!"

Beyond St. Vith at Stavelot, Army Engineers running a saw mill dropped their tools to blow two bridges. But below St. Vith the Germans had opened a 12-mile gap. Three armored divisions including Fritz Bayerlein's reconstituted Panzer Lehr raced to seize Bastogne. No one was there but the headquarters of Troy Middleton's VIII Corps and a few stragglers from the 28th Division. By 10 p.m. December 18 the Germans were only five miles from the town. But Bayerlein got bad advice on which road to take from a Belgian peasant and ended up in a quagmire. The 101st Airborne Division's paratroopers just beat Panzer Lehr to Bastogne that night.

Under intense pressure, Eisenhower decided to transfer the Americans north of what was now a bulge to Montgomery's command. Within two hours Monty was at Hodges's headquarters like, one aide remembers, "Christ come to cleanse the temple." He was full of "Come, come" and "Dear me, this can't go on." But he quickly moved Horrocks's XXX Corps to the Meuse to meet the spearhead of the attack.

Eisenhower met with Bradley and Patton December 19 at the World War I killing ground of Verdun. How soon could Patton wheel his 3rd Army 90 degrees and strike north? Two days, Patton said.

"Don't be fatuous, George," said Eisenhower.

Patton dashed back to his new headquarters in Luxembourg City. "It's either roothog or die," he commanded. "If those sons of bitches want war in the raw, that's the way we'll give it to them. There are to be no reserves. Everybody fights." His tanks were rolling in two days. Col. Walter J. Muller shifted 62,000 tons of supplies in 120 hours and laid 20,000 miles of field wire. In a week the Americans moved 250,000 men and 50,000 vehicles, an unprecedented display of mobility.

In Bastogne, the airborne fought off the panzers which then streamed past the town. "Visualize the hole in the doughnut," explained Lt. Col. Harry Kinnard of the Screaming Eagles. "That's us. So they've got us surrounded, poor bastards."

One regiment of the 101st lost 212 of 600 men in two days. Col. William Roberts, who had fought at Chateau Thierry in the first war and was commanding a few tanks of the 10th Armored, ordered Maj. William Desobry, too young for that war, to hold a road north of Bastogne. "You'll probably be nervous," he counselled. "Then you'll want to pull out. When you begin thinking that, remember I told you NOT to pull out."

Bastogne was encircled by three divisions led by Gen. Hasso von Manteuffel. The Germans in the name of "well-known American humanity" sent a surrender offer under a white flag. "Aw, nuts," said Brig. Gen. Anthony McAuliffe, commander of the 101st troopers. "What the hell should I tell them?"

The weight of American armor was irresistible as it massed to recapture the key village of Houffalize in Belgium.

he asked Kinnard. "The last remark of yours was hard to beat," the colonel responded. "What'd I say?" Reminded, McAuliffe penned a reply for the Germans and history: "To the German Commander/Nuts/The American Commander."

Col. Jospeh Harper took the note to the puzzled Germans. "In plain English it's the same as 'go to hell.' And I'll tell you something else. If you continue to attack, we'll kill every goddamn German that tries to break into the city. On your way, bud," adding for reasons that mystified him, "and good luck to you."

The skies cleared December 23, and the Allies flew 15,000 missions. Some B-26s bombed their own men, who fired back. Other planes dropped supplies on Bastogne where guns were down to 10 rounds each.

The day after Christmas, Col. Creighton Abrams reached the perimeter with 20 tanks and a column of halftracks loaded with infantry. GI lore had it you couldn't serve with Abrams unless you could prove you had killed your own mother and were born out of wedlock. "Let 'er roll," said Abrams, and the siege of Bastogne was history. The impromptu garrison had held up three panzer divisions a crucial three days.

By Christmas Day, the panzers were in sight of the Meuse, 60 miles inside Belgium. Rochefort, on the way to Dinant on the river where Rommel had

scored a brilliant victory four years before, held out two days. Then, on the 28th, tanks of Maj. Gen. Ernest Harmon hit the panzers. The Germans couldn't maneuver. They had run out of gas. The Americans trashed 88 German tanks and captured 75 guns. It was, Harmon reported, "a great slaughter."

Americans were now dug in all over the 60-by-40-mile Bulge. At Bastogne riflemen covered their foxholes with logs. One GI used frozen bodies of Germans. Elsewhere a colonel was told artillery fire he had ordered would land right on his head. "I might as well lose my head. I'm about to lose my ass." Lt. James Creighton of Fox Company of the 26th Division discovered he was leading but his raw recruits weren't following. He ordered his sergeant to shoot any stragglers. The next day they repulsed three German charges. One of their dead was found booby-trapped. So they strung a dead German in a tree in retaliation. When they were finally relieved, only 27 were left of 176 originals. They had learned war.

So did a cook, dragooned into the infantry. "I'll get blown to hell!" he protested. Other cooks and a driver near Wirzfeld knocked out six tanks and killed the infantry behind them. A German ran by the house where Sgt. John Bannister was manning a machine gun on the second floor. "Take a 10-minute break, we'll be back," he shouted in English. "Go to hell! We'll still be here!" Bannister shouted back.

Near Malmedy, 140 men of Battery B 285th Field Artillery had the bad luck to run into Germans. Not

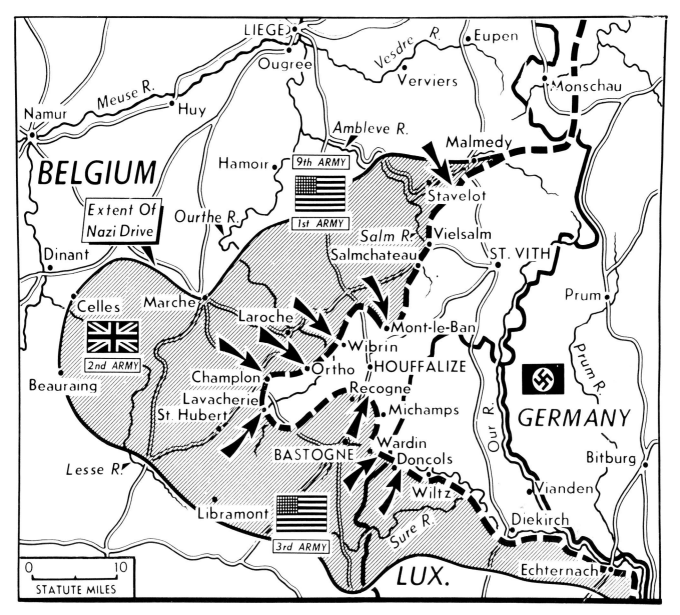

Shaded region indicates the farthest extent of the Bulge before Allied counterattacks began to pinch it shut.

trained in small-arms fighting, they surrendered. As they stood in the snow with their hands up, a German officer commanded: "Kill them all." Ninety-eight were machine-gunned to death. Word quickly spread through the forest. Later Pvt. John

Near Malmedy in the Bulge a battalion of U.S. artillerymen was cut off. Not trained in infantry fighting, they surrendered. Ninety-eight were machine-gunned to death by their German captors.

Fague saw 60 German POWs being marched over a hill. Afterwards he noted 60 dark shapes lying in the snow. Pfc. Kurt Gabel of the 17th Airborne saw two medics shot as they crawled to a wounded GI near Houffalize. He herded some German prisoners ahead of him at gunpoint to retrieve the bodies. That's not in the Geneva Convention, his lieutenant admonished. "Neither is shooting medics."

Rebuffed at the Meuse, Hitler opted for von Rundstedt's "small solution." He also launched an attack in Alsace —Nordwind — hoping to draw Patton back. It didn't work. On New Year's Day, the

Despite German slaughter of U.S. prisoners at Malmedy in the Bulge, these American tankers accepted an enemy surrender. Not all Americans did.

Luftwaffe flew its swan song, an all-out raid that destroyed 134 planes on the ground including Montgomery's personal C-47. But the so-called "Hangover Raid" cost the Germans 220 planes and 300 irreplaceable pilots.

The Americans had fought the Wehrmacht to a standstill. Henry Reath broke open some canned lobster his mother had sent him, added powdered milk and eggs and served his tired men Lobster Newburg.

But where was Monty? Eisenhower wanted him to hit the German flank from the north by January 1. Montgomery said he couldn't move until January 3 and then at the German spearhead. Eisenhower boiled over when, on top of what he considered a lie, Montgomery reopened an old sore by writing him that there should be one offensive from the Bulge. That would be into north Germany, and he, Monty, would lead it. He enclosed such an order.

Glum German prisoners of Hitler's last offensive in the West file past the tanks that defeated them.

Left: *By January 1945 the Allies had flattened out the Bulge. A U.S. tank passing a bogged down buddy, rolls on towards Germany.*

Ike, center, said it couldn't be done. But Patton, right, turned his Third Army in 48 hours to stem Germany's Bulge offensive. Bradley, left, was enraged when Montgomery took the credit.

Ike had only to sign it. Maj. Gen. Freddie de Guingand, Montgomery's aide who was admired at SHAEF as his boss was not, reported back that Ike had moved the 1st Army back to Bradley and was about to fire him. "Who would replace me?" said Monty. Sir Harold Alexander, commander in Italy, said de Guingand then gave Monty an apologetic "Dear Ike" letter he had drafted. Montgomery signed it. That was not the end of it.

January 7 Montgomery held a news conference in Zondhoven, Holland. The first person pronoun predominated... "I took certain steps as soon as I saw what was happening ... I was thinking ahead ... I employed the whole available power of the British group of armies ... very gradually. Finally it was put into play with a bang. I think one of the most interesting and tricky battles I have ever handled."

It was tommyrot, all of it, and left Bradley so incensed he promised: "I cannot serve under Montgomery." If he had to, he fumed, "send me home." Patton, the one whose GIs had provided the "bang," called Monty "a tired little fart. War requires the taking of risks, and he won't take them."

Churchill calmed the storm by telling Parliament it was predominantly an American battle and one of their noblest. And it was.

22

D+335

The thin thread holding the sword of death over Germany snapped January 12, 1945. The Red offensive was overwhelming.

The ages had seen the Golden Horde of Genghis Khan, Tamerlane, the Ottoman Turks sweep out of the Asian steppes. They came for conquest, for pillage, for rapine. This was different. This time the invaders came to avenge 20 million of their fallen countrymen, a dead Russian for every 10 living.

"Two eyes for an eye!" cried party line journalist Ilya Ehrenburg. In southern Poland, Marshal Ivan Konev had massed 300 guns and Katusha rocket launchers per mile. Within a week the Soviets stormed 40 miles, then a Red tide charged forward

Above: Near Grabow in the final days, GI Joe embraces Ivan in a victorious linkup.

Left: A country road in Germany, spring 1945. Death throes of the Third Reich.

on a 500-mile front. Across the frozen rivers they came as Hitler's remaining elite vanished in a storm of smoke and blood. Heinz Guderian, the old tank commader now OKW chief of staff, raged at Hitler to recall 30 divisions from the Baltics before it was too late. Hitler, his body quivering, raged back: no retreat, not one foot. But millions of German refugees took flight to the west before the primal onslaught.

Towns and villages were put to the torch. Factories were dismantled and shipped to Russia. Women were raped, then nailed to cart wheels and bayoneted. Families with photos of Hitler on the wall were butchered. Drunken tankers, their machines bedecked with looted quilts and lined with embroidered pillows, rolled on over anything and anybody in the way.

On January 30, 8,000 terrified refugees jammed aboard the cruise liner Wilhelm Gustloff in Gdynia (now Gdansk). Babes in arms were assured passage,

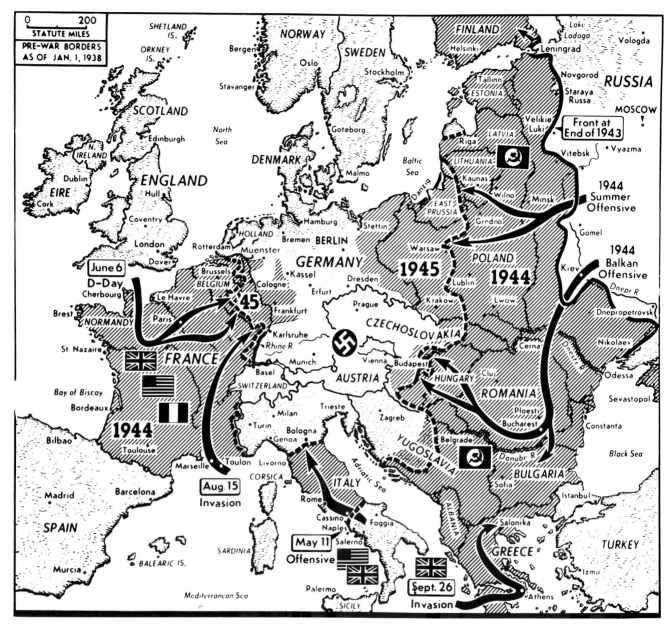

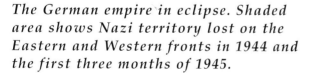

The German empire in eclipse. Shaded area shows Nazi territory lost on the Eastern and Western fronts in 1944 and the first three months of 1945.

so the infants were tossed back to others on the dock so they could board. The next day Russian submarine S13 fired three torpedoes labelled "For the Motherland," "For the Soviet People" and "For Leningrad" into the vessel. Seven thousand drowned.

Out of breath, the Soviet offensive paused at the end of January along the Oder River. Berlin was 35 miles away.

By early in January, the Bulge had been erased.

DRESDEN

The most disputed bombing of the war besides Hiroshima and Nagasaki was the bombing by 1,300 British and American planes of the antique German city of Dresden February 13-14, 1945. As many as 100 thousand died in the resulting firestorm. The RAF said Dresden was a key rail hub — it was not — and a production center — its only munitions factory was outside the bombing area. Churchill said the raid was "a serious query against the conduct of Allied bombing."

Twenty thousand Americans had been killed. Of the 106th, only 4,000 men were not either dead, in hospitals or in POW camps. Patton, who had been dismissed by some as "just a traffic cop" in his dash across France, had fought a classic encirclement in the Saar. By the time the Americans reached the Rhine early in March, they had taken 317,000 prisoners including 25 generals and an admiral.

From his Fuhrerbunker 50 feet below doomed Berlin, Hitler screamed orders to phantom armies that no longer existed. He commanded Albert Speer, his production genius — and he was — to burn the nation.

"What can you do with a people whose men don't fight even when their women are raped?" Hitler ranted. "All the plans, all the ideas of National Socialism are too high, too noble, for such a people." Speer refused to obey. Hitler fired him. Guderian, too.

He had once declared: "Give me five years, and you will not recognize Germany again." True. The Allies did Speer's task for him.

Perhaps nothing has been argued so long about World War II as Eisenhower's policy of not freeing Montgomery to charge to the east across the northern plains of Germany. Monty always insisted he could have reached Berlin first and changed the map of postwar Europe. John Ellis, among many, doesn't buy it. "The more surprising, it seemed, (is) that anyone really believed that the man who waddled tortoise-like behind Rommel in North Africa, who traversed Sicily and (Italy) with if anything more circumspection, should suddenly have been transformed into a dashing amalgam of Frederick the Great and Jeb Stuart."

By way of illustration: after laborious preparation almost down to the last foxhole, Montgomery surged across the Rhine March 23 (Operation Grenade) with 20 divisions and 1,500 tanks accompanied by the best parachute drop of the war. The day before, without any artillery or air power preparation, Patton took advantage of a full moon to cross the Rhine far to the south, suffering only 35 casualties. In fact, he used his rubber assault boats to ferry back German prisoners who were surrendering on the far bank. But neither general was the first over the river.

On March 7 some units of the U.S. 9th Armored Division broke into the Rhine town of Remagen. "My God!" exclaimed Maj. Ben Cothran. There stood the Ludendorff railroad bridge. Intact. It was 3:15 p.m. German prisoners said the bridge would

"ARGONAUT" 1945

Subject: last summit of World War II. Or first of Cold War.

Scene: Yalta February 4-9. Churchill: "We couldn't have found a worse place if we had spent 10 years on a search." Next to war, plumbing main topic of conversation.

George Marshall: "(The Russians) were exceedingly sensitive ... that the British and the Americans were preparing to go off and settle this thing ... We were very careful about this, the Americans more so than the British because Mr. Churchill was quite positive in the matter, and events have proved that he was possibly more nearly right."

Roosevelt, clearly dying, needed Russia as ally to fight Japan, believed Russian occupation of Eastern Europe was a fait accompli and thought, wrongly, Stalin would be placated by keeping conquered territory.

U.S. Military Liaison in Moscow, Maj. Gen. John R. Deane, cautions Marshall: "After the banquets, we send them another 1,000 planes and they approve a visa that has been hanging fire for months. They simply cannot understand giving without taking. Some will say the Red Army won the war for us. I can swallow all of this but the last two words."

Yalta a reputed sellout to Soviets. But: they wanted $20 billion in reparations from Germany. No. Wanted to deindustrialize Germany. No. Wanted much of Poland. No. Wanted southern half of Sakhalin as price for entering Pacific war. Okay.

FDR: giving Russia ancient borders in Poland is like giving the United States back to Great Britain. Summit dismissed.

be blown at 4 o'clock. Lt. Karl Timmermann was ordered to get his men across NOW! Sgt. Alex Drabik and his squad dashed across and set up in some bomb craters. A shell had severed the firing wires to the 500-pound charge of TNT. Within 10 minutes 100 men were across. "Hot dog!" Bradley exulted. Maj. Gen. Harold "Pinky" Bull, Eisen-

The war all but over and their lives all but just begun, these 14-year-olds captured near Berstadt in Germany were nonetheless willing to sacrifice themselves for their Fuhrer.

hower's operations rep with Bradley, protested that the far side wasn't tank country and Remagen wasn't in the plans. "To hell with the planners," said Ike. In five days, several divisions were across before the weakened bridge collapsed. By then pon-

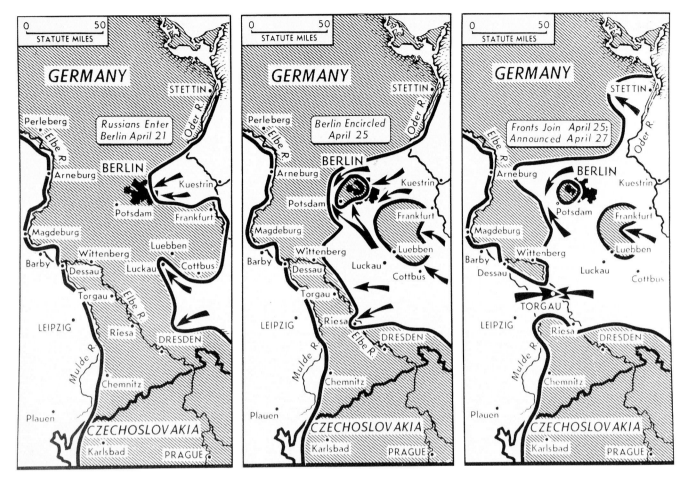

Both East and West fronts join as Berlin is encircled and attacked by Soviet forces.

toon bridges were in place despite some V-2 shots and attack by Luftwaffe jets. Panzer Lehr and the 11th Panzer Division vainly tried to stem the flow. They had four tanks apiece.

Once Eisenhower had said Berlin was the objective. Berlin? "Who would want it?" Ike said now. "I think history will answer that for you," Patton replied. Now his policy was destruction of the German army wherever. A private in the 101st, David Webster, a Harvard lit major, wrote a personal thought home worth wider circulation: "I cannot understand why you hope for a quick end of the war. Unless we take the horror of battle to the Germans, blowing up their houses, smashing open their wine cellars ... unless we litter their streets with horribly rotten German corpses as we did in France, the Germans will prepare for war (again) unmindful of its horrors." And when horrors unimaginable appeared as the Allies reached their heartland, Germans on every hand shook their heads: "We didn't know." The Tommies of the 63rd Anti-Tank Regi-

ment certainly knew as they approached a place called Bergen-Belsen. From a distance it "smelled like a monkey house," said Col. Donald Taylor. Closer it got worse. Then they saw why. A woman holding a dead baby came up to a soldier, pleading for milk. He humored her by spooning some at the infant. Then the mother fell dead. Inside were more living skeletons and many more dead ones. The 4th Armored found another camp at Ohrdruf. The enraged Americans forced the mayor and his wife to walk through the camp. They went home and hanged themselves.

Who knew what and for how long about Hitler's Final Solution is a profound question of international morality that has never been unequivocally answered. Word of what was happening at Auschwitz had reached the Warsaw ghetto early on from two escapees. Aerial photos had been taken of the death camp. After the war the Allies said they didn't want to bomb it for fear, paradoxically, of killing innocent civilians. When Russian troops liberated

Maidenek in July 1944, a correspondent sent word to a disbelieving Herald Tribune in New York which decided "... this sounds inconceivable." Auschwitz, freed in January 1945 by the Soviet offensive, dispelled any doubt. "If the heavens were paper and all the water in the world ink, and all the trees were turned into pens, you could not even then record the sufferings and the horrors," said one rabbi.

Not always did the Jews go stoically to their deaths. When 2,100 SS soldiers marched into the Warsaw ghetto April 19, 1943, to round up the last 50,000 survivors of the original 400,000 Jews herded behind the ghetto walls, they were met with fierce resistance. Armed with only two submachine guns, 17 rifles and several hundred pistols, the Jews drove the SS troopers out. They returned with flame throwers, artillery and poison gas and relentlessly turned the ghetto into "one huge cemetery." Some 7,000 Jews died in the fighting, which lasted until September when the last resistance in the rubble ended. The surviving Jews were shipped to Treblinka to be gassed.

An uprising burned Treblinka in August 1943. There was a revolt in Sobibor that October, and a number of Jews escaped and joined the partisans. And there was stoic dignity. Elder Jacob Edelstein rebuked an SS officer about to kill him at Auschwitz. "Of the last moments on this earth I am the master, not you." He turned to pray, then: "Now I am ready."

But the killing continued to the end. On his last visit to Theresienstadt April 10, 1943, Eichmann declared: "I shall gladly jump into the pit knowing that in the same pit there are five million enemies of the state." As the invaders neared the camps, the insanity persisted. The starving inmates were forced on marches to who knew where away from the front. So near but so far from rescue, thousands were shot.

Young Samuel Pisar managed to escape from Dachau. Some miles away he came upon a tank with a star on its turret. The first black man he had ever seen emerged. Pisar hugged the man around his knees and spoke the few English words his mother had taught him: "God bless America." Then: "He

At Allied insistence, some burghers of Buchenwald view the evidence of what went on outside their town.

East meets West as American and Russian soldiers shake hands across a ruined bridge over the Elbe near Torgau. It is April 15, 1945.

picked me up and took me with him through the hatch and into the womb of freedom."

In April, Eisenhower went to Ohrdruf to see for himself. Patton stepped aside to vomit. Eisenhower said he had come "in order to be in a position to give first-hand evidence of these things if ever in the future there develops a tendency to charge these allegations to propaganda." He saw the still-smoking crematoria, heaped bodies, butcher blocks where jaws were smashed to remove gold fillings.

He stood where menstruating women were given pads soaked in gasoline that were then set afire.

"I want every American unit not actually on the front lines to see this place. We are told that the American soldier does not know what he is fighting for. Now at least he will see what he is fighting against." Edward R. Murrow broadcast from Buchenwald shaking with rage: "I pray you believe what I have said...(but) for most of it I have no words."

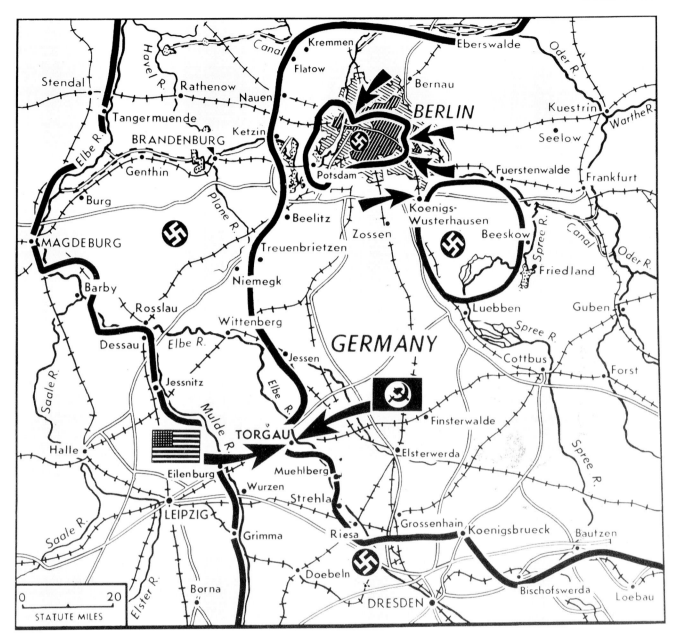

Close-up of union of Allied forces while Hitler's last stand takes place at Berlin.

It was springtime in Bavaria. Sgt. John Baldwin, a chaplain's assistant in the 42nd "Rainbow" Division and a choirmaster in civilian life, spotted a steeple in the distance. Thinking there might be an organ in the church, he drove his requisitioned Volkswagen scout car over. The Catholic priest fed him a breakfast of homemade bread and ham, then said: "My people don't know anything about the *lager*."

"*Lager*," Baldwin thought. "What's *lager*?" The 42nd soon discovered. They stumbled upon Dachau. "There was pandemonium," said Baldwin. "These skeletons were all over us, hugging us. We gave them an hour with the guards. They mutilated them, castrated them. We were stunned. What was this? They dragged us to the furnaces. We still didn't understand."

The 42nd soon moved on, leaving the camp to follow-up troops. Baldwin still has a cattle whip taken from one of the guards.

The Russians began the final assault on Berlin April 16 with a titanic barrage by 40,000 guns. Anyone retreating would be shot, Hitler commanded. Many actually obeyed and died where they fought.

Trapped in his bunker and in his own fury of

Did he know what he was signing, Eisenhower asked Col. Gen. Alfred Jodl as he affixed his name to surrender at a Rheims schoolhouse May 7, 1945. "Ja," the Nazi chief of staff replied.

unreality, Hitler raged: "The war is lost!" He named Doenitz to be his successor, ordered Goering arrested in the mistaken belief he had staged a coup and had SS Maj. Gen. Hermann Fegelin, Eva Braun's brother-in-law, shot when he was found in Berlin in civilian clothes. Then, in a macabre display of bourgeois morality, he had a petty city official found fighting in the rubble brought to the bunker to marry himself and his mistress. The official was killed returning to his post. The wedding party sipped champagne, the groom Tokay. He wrote his last testament, assailing to the end "the universal poisoner of all nations, international Jewry."

Two days later, April 30, he tried out a cyanide capsule on his pet German shepherd, Blondi. The dog died instantly. Then he and Eva withdrew to his room in the bunker. Aides heard a shot. They found her curled on a couch, dead. She had taken cyanide. Hitler was slumped at a table, a hole in his forehead from his favorite 7.65 mm Walther pistol, the gun he had carried so long ago in the Burgerbraukeller in Munich. Nearby in a silver frame was a photo of his mother as a young woman. The bodies were cremated. As if in memoriam, 1,000 Jews were shot that same day as they were herded from Theresienstadt.

The next day Goebbels and his wife gave the poisoned pills to their six children, then had SS officers shoot them. In Italy, communist partisans caught Mussolini and his mistress, Clara Petacci, near Como as they tried to reach Switzerland, shot them and hung the bodies upside down in a gas station in Milan after vengeful men and women spat and urinated on them. An English soldier decorously pinned up Petacci's skirt.

On April 25, Lt. Albert Kotzebue of the 69th Division on patrol near the Elbe River spotted a lone Russian horseman outside the village of Strehla. The Allies had linked up. Germans by the thousands swam across to surrender to the Americans instead of the Russians. An American GI escorting 68 POWs down a road wound up with 1,200. "Every house you passed had a white sheet hanging in the window," said Brad Cochran of the 99th. Alan Moorehead noted the discolored spot on living room walls where Hitler's portrait had recently hung.

German resistance in the west crumbled. "Every once in a while a few of the fanatics would blow up the first jeep to enter a town," said John Lyman, the Harvard lawyer-gunner. "Our usual response was to haul back and paste the town with white phosphorous, blow the son of a bitch up and burn it down. Then the villagers would ask us to put out the fire. We'd tell them, 'Tough luck, Mac. You should have thought of that before you killed our guys.'"

Gordon Carson motored down an autobahn with the 101st. "As far as you could see were German prisoners fully armed. We just waved."

FDR
1882-1945

Seeking a rest, Roosevelt arrived at Warm Springs, Georgia, March 30, 1945. Stationmaster C.A. Pless said the President was "the worst looking man I ever saw who was still alive." On April 12 he was posing in a suit with his old Harvard school tie for portraitist Elizabeth Shoumantoff. The picture was to be a gift for the daughter of his mistress of 30 years, Lucy Mercer Rutherfurd, who was in the room with him.

For months Roosevelt had been unable even to shave himself. But that morning he had breakfasted well on fried eggs, bacon and toast, then read the Atlanta paper before the artist arrived. He gave her 15 minutes more before lunch, then said his last words: "I have a terrific headache." A stroke was killing him. He, who had taken office 10 days before Hitler, died 18 days before him. A mourning nation wondered what to make of a seemingly lesser politician named Harry S. Truman.

Simpson's 9th Army reached the Elbe April 15. He said he had an open road to Berlin 45 miles away. Bradley ordered him to stop. "We're going to Berlin," said a jubilant Brig. Gen. Sidney R. Hinds of the 2nd Armored. Simpson was long silent, then said: "We're not going to Berlin, Sid. This is the end of the war for us."

Patton had driven into Bavaria in pursuit of an unfounded belief that Hitler planned a last stand there. On May 4 he entered Czechoslovakia and begged permission to go on to Prague which had not been covered by the occupation agreement at Yalta. Ike asked the Russians. Please don't, they replied. Patton's tanks were finally stopped.

On May 2, Kesselring surrendered the army in Italy after negotiating a month with Allen Dulles of the OSS in Switzerland. Shortly after, the U.S. 88th Division in Italy met up with the 103rd Division out of Germany near the Brenner Pass.

Men of the 101st raced up the alpine road to Hitler's retreat at Berchtesgaden, bombed to smithereens. But his Mercedes-Benz limousines were intact. The paratroopers shot at the windows to see if

Field marshal's baton shining to the end, Gerd von Rundstedt is questioned by Lt. Gen. Alexander Patch shortly after the capture of the man who led the Nazi armies in France and in the Bulge.

they were bullet proof, then joy-rode about until officers pulled rank and commandeered the cars. One spiteful GI drained the radiator of his before turning it over.

On May 5, Adm. Hans-Georg von Friedberg was escorted to a boys' school in Rheims and began negotiating along with Jodl in a recreation room where students used to play ping-pong and chess. Jodl balked. Eisenhower told him if he didn't sign the surrender, the Americans would stop accepting German prisoners, leaving them to the mercy of the Russians. At 2:39 a.m. May 7, Jodl signed the surrender for Doenitz. Bedell Smith signed for Eisenhower.

The Supreme Commander then met with Jodl. Did the German understand what he had signed, Eisenhower asked icily. "Ja, ja," Jodl answered. The war was over.

Eisenhower gathered his weary staff and offered some champagne. It was flat. He asked if anyone had an idea for a victory statement. Nothing brilliant was offered. So the small-town soldier from Abilene wrote his own:

"The mission of this Allied force was fulfilled at 0241 local time May 7, 1945."

Then he called Bradley at the Fuhrstenhof Hotel at Bad Wildungen. Bradley took out his map case and wrote on a new page: D+335.

23

DETROIT

So what, in the end, did it all prove?
No body count exists or is possible.

Not from the ashes of nameless Jews used in the winter on icy walkways at Auschwitz.

Not from mangled remains in the basements of the moonscape of Stalingrad.

Not from the furtive killing pits now overgrown in eastern Poland.

Not from the cinders of Dresden or Hiroshima or Berlin. Not from the burning lanes of London.

Not from the sands of North Africa long since drifted over the tracks of those who passed by.

Not from the rocks of Italy long ago washed by the rain of blood if not memory.

Not from the tide-lines of so many beaches where bodies rolled in the surf.

A workman directs tank treads for M-10 tank destroyers at a Ford Plant in Highland Park, Michigan.

CAUTION! MAXIMUM CAPACITY OF THIS BEAM 3500 LBS.

Workers at an ordnance loading plant in Philadelphia stack 500 pound bombs in a railway freight car.

Not from the fathomless graveyard of the North Atlantic.

The common estimate is that somewhere between 50 and 55 million human beings died in World War II. Ask again: for what?

Hardly had the guns cooled than another war began that was to disfigure the map of Europe for almost half a century. As Versailles had begot World War II, so World War II begot the Cold War between the Soviet Union and its former partners of the West. And in the bitterest of ironies, the defeated Axis allies, Japan and Germany, rose from the ashes to an economic preeminence achieved peacefully beyond anything they had gained at gunpoint. Then why had the millions died?

Many historians resist the "great man" theory, that one person can determine events of such mag-

Previous pages: *An assembly line for Grumman Wildcat fighter planes.*

nitude. It is legitimate, however, to ask what might have happened — or not happened — had Hitler been killed in his Beer Hall Putsch? If the French had stiffened over the Rhineland? If the Allies, not all that much less prepared than Hitler in 1938, had said "no further" at Munich? Versailles had created his stage, but Adolf Hitler certainly directed the godforsaken scenario that followed.

In "The Gathering Storm," one of his volumes of the war's history, Churchill wrote: "One day President Roosevelt told me he was asking publicly for suggestions about what the war should be called. I said at once 'the Unnecessary War.' There never was a war more easy to stop than that which had just wrecked what was left of the world from the previous struggle."

There had been chances, not taken, to stop Hitler. And if he had been stopped, would Japan have taken the leap into the abyss without him? Quite possibly not.

"What if?" cannot substitute for "what was." Probably not even Hitler himself knew what he had in mind in the future for a subject Europe. But what he displayed once in power more than justified — it demanded — the war to overthrow his fanatic and bloody-minded regime. Churchill saw this more clearly, and sooner, than most. He is the hero of the piece. Roosevelt, too, had the vision — but not, at first, the political leeway — to see that Europe's war was also America's. Stalin had no alternative but to fight for survival, then, that won, for hegemony.

Hitler is the puzzle. It is possible he did not truly understand modern war. Factory lines are more of a determinant than the front lines. His Luftwaffe Chief of Staff, Gen. Hans Jeschonnek, and not he alone, perceived this early on. He bluntly predicted: "If we have not won the war by December 1942, we have no prospect of doing so." After defeats in Tunisia, at Kursk, in Sicily, at Midway and Guadalcanal in the Pacific and as Italy was being invaded, a Japanese diplomat in Lisbon said: "It is generally considered here that the eventual outcome of the war is settled, and it is now only a question of time."

Yet Hitler kept clutching at the straws of secret weapons. Ironically, the one decisive weapon within his grasp was one he never really pursued. The Germans had split the atom in 1938, the first scientists to do so. Their physicists were as good as any in the world. But while the Anglo-Americans em-

Anti-aircraft guns pointing skyward being built at a General Motors factory.

barked on a frantic effort to develop a nuclear weapon before Hitler did, he never assigned the idea much priority. A recent book by Thomas Powers suggests that Werner Heisenberg, head of German atomic research, may have intentionally dragged his feet on perfecting a bomb. Americans found to their surprise in 1945, and relief, that the Germans had gone no farther than working on an

energy-producing atomic pile, something Enrico Fermi had achieved in Chicago almost three years earlier.

Hitler lacked long-term plans. The Americans, on the other hand, won the war with an army remarkably close to Wedemeyer's prewar estimate of what it would take. The United States raised 89 divisions in World War II. Only two were never committed to action.

The Soviet Union and Germany just kept throwing more flesh into the cauldron. Eleven million Soviet soldiers died and 3.5 million Germans. And 1.3 million Japanese. The Americans lost 292,131

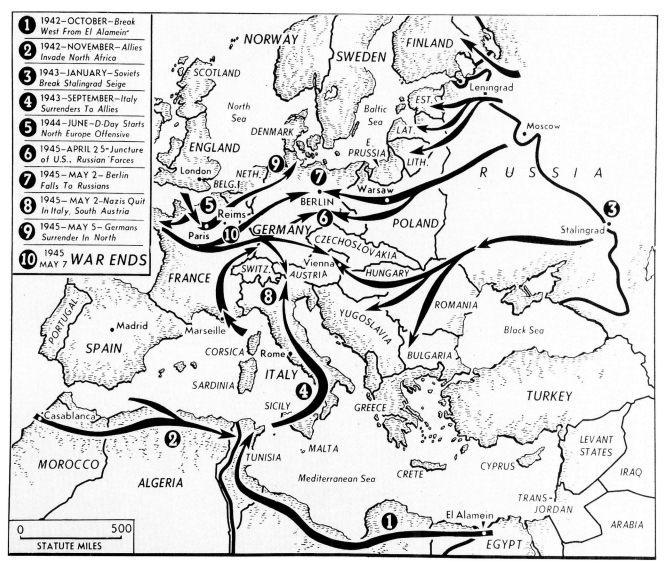

Progress of World War II in Europe from El Alamein to its conclusion on May 7, 1945.

lives, the British 264,443. Civilians suffered proportionately: 7 million Russian dead, 780,000 Germans, 672,000 Japanese, 60,000 British. And it was civilians who were essential to victory by making the weapons of modern war.

America's Depression-racked factories did, indeed, become arsenals. Four million women joined the workforce, and Rosie the Riveter's hands became as famous as Betty Grable's legs. The assembly line in Ford's massive Willow Run bomber plant was 40 percent female. Sylvania's production lines making delicate proximity fuses were all women because of their greater dexterity. Even manicurists were hired to file delicate parts.

Dependent as he was on slave labor, Hitler never grasped the decisive productive capacity of a free people, that the lathe was as mighty as the sword.

By the end of 1942, concluded the U.S. Strategic Bombing Survey: "The outcome no longer depended on skillful strategy and well-timed shock effect. Germany could not hope to win. It was becoming, instead, a war in which military manpower and economic resources would be decisive." That is, the deep pockets of Soviet blood and American steel.

Between 1942 and 1945, the Allies produced *more* than Germany: 156,000 tanks and self-propelled guns, 4.07 million machine guns, 400,248 planes including 133,000 fighters. They outproduced the Axis 7:1 in steel, 47:1 in oil. The United States built 137 aircraft carriers of various sizes, Japan 13.

"In the final analysis," writes John Ellis, "once America and Russia had been drawn into the war and once each had blocked its opponent's first mad rush, then there was absolutely no chance that the Axis powers could salvage even a negotiated peace ... A Reich that would wage a blitzkrieg war with only 47,000 tanks versus its enemy's 227,000, 116,000 guns versus 915,000 and 350,000 trucks versus 3 million, or a would-be maritime power (Japan) that aims to maintain its grasp by producing only 13 carriers to its opponent's 137 has not much real chance of imposing its will.... Many battlefields have been cited as being particularly significant for Germany's defeat in World War II. Not the least of them should be Detroit."

Adm. Yamamoto had visited Detroit's assembly lines while a naval attache in Washington. It was why he forecast Japan had only a brief time to "run wild." It was the world's tragedy that Adolf Hitler had never been there.

Gen. Jeschonnek had sensed the winds. As 1942 passed, Germany had not won the war. He committed suicide. Surrounded by the flames of this "unnecessary" war, Hitler, of course, did likewise. But by then it was far too late to matter.

BIBLIOGRAPHY

Adelson, Alan & Lapides, Robert, eds., *Lodz Ghetto.* Penguin, London, 1989.

Ambrose, Stephen E., *The Supreme Commander.* Doubleday, New York, 1969.

—-, *Band of Brothers.* Simon & Schuster, New York, 1992.

Blumenson, Martin, *Kasserine Pass.* Houghton Mifflin, Boston, 1967.

Brown, Anthony Cave, *Bodyguard of Lies.* Harper & Row, New York, 1975.

Browning, Christopher R., *Ordinary Men.* Harper Collins, New York, 1992.

Carse, Robert, *Dunkirk:1940.* Prentice-Hall, Englewood Cliffs, New Jersey, 1970.

Casdorph, Paul D., *Let the Good Times Roll.* Paragon, New York, 1991.

Cole, Wayne S. *Charles A. Lindbergh and the Battle Against Intervention.* Harcourt, Brace, Jovanovich, New York, 1974.

Collier, Richard, *The Freedom Road.* Atheneum, New York, 1984.

Davis, Kenneth S., *Experience of War.* Doubleday, Garden City, New York, 1965.

Duffy, Christopher, *Red Storm on the Reich.* Atheneum, New York, 1991.

Ellis, John, *Brute Force.* Penquin, London, 1990.

D'Este, Carlo, *Bitter Victory.* Dutton, New York, 1988.

Fleming, Peter, *Operation Sea Lion.* Simon & Schuster, New York, 1957.

Fussell, Paul, *Wartime.* Oxford, New York, 1989.

Gilbert, Martin, *The Holocaust.* Holt, Rinehart & Winston, New York, 1985.

Goralski, Robert, *World War II Almanac.* G.P. Putnam's Sons, New York, 1981.

Goutard, Col. A., *The Battle of France: 1940.* Ives Washburn, New York, 1959.

Hapgood, David & Richardson, David, *Monte Cassino.* Congdon & Weed, New York, 1984.

Hastings, Max, *Overlord.* Simon and Schuster, New York, 1984.

Hodgson, Godfrey, *The Colonel: The Life and Wars of Henry Stimson.* Knopf, New York, 1990.

Holt, Nicholas Bethell, *The War HItler Won.* Holt, Rinehart & Winston, New York, 1989.

Horne, Alistair, *To Lose a Battle.* Little, Brown, Boston, 1969.

Hough, Richard & Richards, Denis, *The Battle of Britan.* Norton, New York, 1989.

Hoyt, Edwin P., *The GI's War.* McGraw-Hill, New York, 1988.

Liddell Hart, B.H., *History of the Second World War.* Putnam, New York, 1971.

Keegan, John, *Six Armies in Normandy.* Viking, New York, 1984.

Keitl, Field Marshal Wilhelm, *Memoirs.* Stein & Day, New York, 1966.

Ketchum, Richard M., *The Borrowed Years: 1938-1941.* Random House, New York, 1989.

Kennett, Lee, *GI.* Scribner's, New York, 1987.

Klingman, William K., *1941.* Harper & Row, New York, 1988.

Larrabee, Eric, *Commander in Chief.* Simon & Schuster, New York, 1987.

Leckie, Robert, *Delivered From Evil.* Harper & Row, New York, 1987.

Lord, Walter, *The Miracle of Dunkirk.* Viking, New York, 1982.

Manchester, William, *The Glory and the Dream.* Little, Brown, Boston, 1974.

Moorehead, Alan, *Eclipse.* Harper & Row, New York, 1968.

Morris, Eric, *Salerno.* Stein & Day, New York, 1983.

Mosley, Leonard, *Marshall: Hero for Our Times.* Hearst, New York, 1982.

Nichols, David, ed., *Ernie's War.* Random House, New York, 1986.

Patrick, Stephen A., *The Normandy Campaign.* W.H. Smith, New York, 1986.

Pogue, Forrest C., *George C. Marshall: Ordeal and Hope.* Viking, New York, 1966.

—-, *George C. Marshall: Organizer of Victory.* Viking, New York, 1973.

Ryan, Cornelius, *The Longest Day.* Simon & Schuster, New York 1959.

—-, *A Bridge Too Far.* Simon & Schuster, New York, 1974.

Salisbury, Harrison, *900 Days: The Siege of Leningrad.* Harper & Row, New York, 1969.

Scott, George, *Rise and Fall of the League of Nations.* London, 1973.

Sears, Stephen W. ed., *Eyewitness to World War II.* 2 vols. Houghton Mifflin, Boston, 1991.

Shachtman, Tom, *The Phoney War.* Harper & Row, New York, 1982.

Shirer, William L., *The Rise and Fall of the Third Reich.* Simon & Schuster, New York, 1960.

Toland, John, *Adolf Hitler.* Doubleday, Garden City, New York, 1976.

van der Val, Dan, *The Atlantic Campaign.* Harper & Row, New York, 1988.

Watt, Donald Cameron, *How War Came.* Pantheon, New York, 1989.

Werth, Alexander, *Russia at War.* Dutton, New York, 1964.

Young, Brig. Peter, *World Almanac of World War II.* Pharos Books, New York, 1981.

Oral History

Family histories, Stephen W. Parker

Interviews

John Baldwin, Joseph Cagney, Bradford Cochran, Henry Reath, P.K. Smith